ZONE OF THE INTERIOR

ZONE OF THE INTERIOR

A Memoir, 1942–1947

D ANIEL H OFFMAN

LOUISIANA STATE UNIVERSITY PRESS

Baton Rouge   MM

First printing
09 08 07 06 05 04 03 02 01 00
5 4 3 2 1

Designer: Amanda McDonald Scallan
Typeface: Bembo
Printer and binder: Thomson-Shore, Inc.

Library of Congress Cataloging-in-Publication Data

Hoffman, Daniel, 1923–
    Zone of the interior : a memoir, 1942–1947 / Daniel Hoffman.
        p. cm.

    ISBN 0-8071-2568-7 (cloth : perm. paper)
    1. Hoffman, Daniel, 1923– 2. World War, 1939–1945—Aerial operations,
American. 3. World War, 1939–1945—Personal narratives, American. 4.
United States. Army Air Forces—Biography. 5. Airmen—United
States—Biography. 6. Poets, American—20th century—Biography. I.
Title.
    D790 .H64 2000
    940.54'4973'092—dc21
                                                            99-050733

The paper in this book meets the guidelines for permanence and durability of the Committee on Production
Guidelines for Book Longevity of the Council on Library Resources. ∞

*To those who flew and kept in flight
the P-47C and the B-17F*

BOOKS BY DANIEL HOFFMAN

POETRY

An Armada of Thirty Whales
A Little Geste
The City of Satisfactions
Striking the Stones
Broken Laws
The Center of Attention
Brotherly Love
Hang-Gliding from Helicon: New and Selected Poems, 1948–1988
Middens of the Tribe

CRITICISM

Paul Bunyan, Last of the Frontier Demigods
The Poetry of Stephen Crane
Form and Fable in American Fiction
Barbarous Knowledge: Myth in the Poetry of Yeats, Graves, and Muir
Poe Poe Poe Poe Poe Poe Poe
Faulkner's Country Matters
Words to Create a World: Essays, Interviews, and Reviews of Contemporary Poetry

AS EDITOR

The Red Badge of Courage and Other Tales
American Poetry and Poetics
(With Samuel Hynes) *English Literary Criticism: Romantic and Victorian*
Harvard Guide to Contemporary American Writing
Ezra Pound and William Carlos Williams

Contents

Preface

IN this memoir of my experiences between 1942 and 1947, if, as in the ballad of Lillie Mae Hartley, "some's all true and some but partly," any deviations from the factual result from the fraying of memory over more than fifty years. I have tried accurately to reconstruct how the chance of a summer job after my sophomore year in college put me in the vanguard of a profession the military application of which led to my assignment to Headquarters, Materiel Command (later designated Air Technical Service Command) at Wright Field in Dayton, Ohio.

In the military parlance of the Second World War the world was divided into three parts: the European Theater, the Pacific Theater, and the Zone of the Interior. The last of these terms described duty within the continental United States, where, as its designation suggests, military life was considered to be more passive than what was required in theaters of operations.

It is generally accepted that wartime service was the defining experience for those who survived it, as attested by many personal memoirs, novels, and motion pictures. All such documents that come to mind record the testing of character in battle. Yet of the over 11 million persons in the Army, at least half saw no combat; on April 30, 1945, at the war's end, the total Army personnel numbered 8,290,993, of whom 2,307,501 were in the Army Air Forces, and of the total number, 60.4 percent, some 5 million, "were deployed in the principal overseas theaters," though of course not all saw combat. The remaining nearly 40 percent, over 3,283,000, served in the United States in support of the troops at the front, behind the lines—very far behind the lines indeed. (Robert R. Palmer and Bell I. Wiley, *The Organization of Ground Combat Troops [United States Army in World War II: The Army Ground Forces],* Washington, D.C.: Historical Division, U.S. Army, 1947.)

Nonetheless, for these noncombatants, too, the war was the defining experience of their generation. For many, perhaps for most, stateside service involved the boredom of make-work duty at isolated bases; my lot was different. The experiences recorded here suggest how, even from the lowly perspective of an enlisted man and lieutenant, an Army Air Force Headquarters in the Zone of the Interior was a paradigm of the industrial complex the military was assigned to defend and designed to resemble. The summer job described in the first part of this memoir immerses the young college student in an unexpected niche of that military-industrial complex.

In the event, the tasks I was assigned in both the civilian job I held in 1942–43 and in the Army Air Force, 1943–46, involved the writing, editing, and production, first, of aircraft instruction manuals, and then of a review of scientific and engineering progress unique to that time. These publications have long been dispersed and discarded—an Internet search of the library catalogs at major schools of engineering found none that has preserved them; since, as government publications, they required no copyright, neither were they were deposited in the Library of Congress. My inquiry to the library at Wright-Patterson Field elicited no response. So there is no record of the problems of the recording, condensing, and distributing technical information faced by the Army Air Force for which, in those days so long before the present technologies of the Information Age, comparatively primitive measures were offered as solutions. With the thought that what I can describe may interest readers concerned with such developments, I have set down what I can recall.

★   ★   ★

If the term *Zone of the Interior* be borrowed from military jargon and applied to what Whitman called "a single separate person," it can designate a psychological delving, an exploration of the inner life of one discovering who he is. That, too, is part of a defining experience. In this case, as the center of that inner life involves the search for emotional and intellectual roots and the need to write poems, the quest for identity in the context of military technology becomes a double life, one in each of what C. P. Snow described as our two cultures.

I kept no diaries but have had recourse to letters sent to my late parents, to copies of several memoranda I prepared while in service, and to a file of the publications discussed in the memoir. These were useful in corroborating details. Should any errors of omission or of fact involve anyone named herein, I can but hope that my good intentions, though flawed, will win forgiveness for unintended inaccuracies.

Swarthmore, Pennsylvania

Acknowledgments

I owe thanks to my first readers—to Edward T. Chase for his helpful suggestions, to Philip Beidler and the late Monroe K. Spears for their encouragement, and to Leon Goldin for his reality check on my memories of Wright Field. Professor Russell F. Weigley of the Center for the Study of Force and Diplomacy, Temple University, provided the figures on military service quoted above. Nina D. Myatt of the Olive Kettering Library, Antioch College, offered helpful corroboration of my recollections of a rally nearby for Gerald L. K. Smith, and Freda Barry Brown shared remembrances of our days at the Jordanoff Aviation Company. Thanks also to my editor, Gerry Anders, especially for finding a resource that correctly identified the Natter (Viper), the German rocket-powered interceptor I had always remembered as the "Nadir," as we (mis)pronounced it at Wright Field.

All of my poems in this memoir save two are reprinted from *Hang-Gliding from Helicon: New and Selected Poems, 1948–1988* (Baton Rouge: Louisiana State University Press, 1988). The exceptions are "The Ballad of Lillie May Hartley," here published for the first time, and "In Memory of Lewis Corey," from my book *Broken Laws* (New York: Oxford University Press, 1970). Prose quotations are acknowledged in the text.

ZONE OF THE INTERIOR

I

FINGERPRINTED, photographed, and cleared by the F.B.I., on an early morning in June 1942, the air still cool and dewy, I felt the wind on my face as Sidney Senzer drove his open roadster along a speedway on Long Island toward Farmingdale, where we would show our clearances to an armed sentry and enter the Republic Aviation Company's parking lot, beside the huge hangar where a still-secret fighter plane was being assembled. Sidney was editor-in-chief at Jordanoff Aviation—actually, the only editor they had—and I, newly hired, was his Boy Friday. I had no title. My job was to carry his notebook and portable Corona typewriter (the model with only three rows of keys and a carriage that folded back over the keys to fit into its little black case) and help in any way he asked while he took notes on the project. Which was, to work up a manual of instructions for the pilot to fly, and another for mechanics to service, a huge fighter plane with .50-caliber machine guns mounted in its wings.

Sid Senzer was as new to his job as I was to mine. He had recently been let go as account executive by Foote, Cone and

Belding; changes in wartime economies had affected the advertising business, and his accounts had vanished, his longtime job
with them. His special talent was for devising vivid visual presentations, but he'd been trained at M.I.T as an engineer—a field
in which he'd never held a job because, he told me, of the anti-
Semitism rampant in engineering firms at the time. Perhaps the
Depression had something to do with it too. In any case, suddenly at liberty, he had found an ad in the *New York Times* for an
experienced writer with technical background, and now was editor-in-chief of a firm that had four employees, of whom I was
one.

This was my summer job, after my sophomore year as a pre-
engineering student at Columbia. The summer before, I'd
worked in my Uncle Charlie's small plant, Davies Air-Conditioning. I spent eight hours a day pushing a foot-pedal on a press
that bent metal sheets which, when riveted together, formed air
ducts to be installed in destroyers. The score of regular employees, an amiable crew of middle-aged Italians and Jews, had a ban-
tering camaraderie and during lunch hours would tune in to
WNYC or WQXR for symphonies, quartets, or better still, op-
eratic arias. This factory was on the second floor of a building
next to the East River in the 20s, where the street looked like
the set for the movie *Dead End Kids.* Out in the street, near its
dead end, were the kids.

My freshman summer spent thus was, I felt, enough experience of mindless physical labor, so at the end of sophomore year
I applied to the college placement bureau for something more
stimulating, anything that might draw on my training. While
waiting for such a dream assignment to turn up in my mail, I
learned from my mother that the husband of her friend Ann
Senzer had just taken a new job, some kind of aeronautical editing; it involved fieldwork, and since Sidney had a heart condition
and the job looked to be strenuous, she was hoping his employer
would agree to hire him an assistant. On learning of this I wrote
him, volunteering to be considered for the job if there was one,
and had the placement office send my dossier in the hope that
my being listed as a pre-engineer with good grades in English
and Humanities would be an advantage.

After two years of pre-engineering—actually only one, since freshman year was mostly occupied with required courses in Humanities and Contemporary Civilization—I was no stellar candidate. My favorite engineering course was mechanical drawing, but in that I got only a C−. In math I was swiftly out of my depth, assuredly not one of the few Clever Dicks in Professor L. Parker Siceloff's class in analytic geometry who could answer his poser: Bell Telephone uses cables of various diameters, wound on spools of 2,000 yards. Several of these spools are partially used. How can Bell calculate the remaining yardage? In vain I pulled my ear on this conundrum, trying to figure how to calculate the diameters and consequent lengths of half-wound spools of cables of differing thicknesses, an impossible task. Never did I dream of the obvious: *weigh* the unused spools, then the used ones, and compare. I wonder did any of my classmates realize—I surely didn't until years afterwards—that this conundrum had little to do with math but required nonmathematical analytical thinking. In the event, the following semester I had to drop out of integral calculus after mononucleosis brought me to a standstill; the first term of sophomore year I took it again, passed the weekly quizzes but flunked the final. It was becoming obvious that I was fated to be a suppliant of the Mistress of Words, not a thane of the Master of Numbers.

Still, I persisted in pre-engineering. The most distinguished acquaintance of my family's was Lazarus White, who had been consulted by the Italian government on how to keep the Leaning Tower of Pisa from falling down, and whose firm, Spencer, White and Prentiss, had built New York subway lines. And at New Rochelle High School it was my science teachers, two men who were also adjunct professors (Mr. Hussey of physics, Dr. Spear of chemistry) at the College of New Rochelle, who treated their students as mature persons with serious interests in their subjects. These were my role models. Miss Newell gave me great encouragement in English, for I was one of the few pupils who had any enthusiasm for the readings she assigned from *The Idylls of the King,* or "My Last Duchess" or "Ode to the West Wind." As for contemporary poets, we read strophes by Sandburg and Amy Lowell, and Adelaide Crapsey's cinquains. I was early attracted to poems, going back to nursery rhymes and the chants of children's games—these were my first experiences of folk poetry, though of course I didn't know that then. Reading poems in the grade school and high school text anthologies—the physical rhythms of their language, the evocation of experiences not otherwise dreamed of, the sounds of words rhyming with one another, and the ways such patterns brought forth emotions—all seized my imagination and invited efforts at emulation. I got up my nerve to show Miss Newell some imitative rhymes I had eked out, and she was the first to encourage me to think seriously of writing poems. But how could that lead to a career? College was to prepare me for a career. I signed on for pre-engineering.

At the end of the 1930s, the Depression was not over. My family still faced hard times. So I applied for a scholarship to the University of Rochester, given to students with the highest average of scores on the state Regents examinations. Losing out by a fraction of a point, I went instead to Columbia, where my father had to provide tuition ($400 per year) and my living expenses. I pitched in with part-time jobs, waiting on tables, helping tenants about to move pack their belongings and clean their apartments, and hiring out as an amateur detective to a suspicious husband whose lawyer required a log of his wife's activities while the husband was at work. The hourly pay was nugatory. About all I learned from these employments was how the numbers racket operated, since my perusal of Mrs. X required that I stand for hours, pretending to be an art student sketching the fronts of brownstones, on a corner of Columbus Avenue much frequented by swarthy men bearing paper bags who darted in and out of a candy store otherwise visited only by schoolchildren.

These were make-work jobs. My career goal was industrial engineering, a branch of the profession I thought would be less demanding than those more firmly welded to hard sciences: electrical, mechanical, civil, and hydraulic engineering. In the hard sciences I was as baffled as in math. In Professor Carpenter's Inorganic Chemistry I struggled with the table of elements, memorizing symbols and valences to little avail. More memorable than those was the student in the top row of the amphitheater where Carpenter lectured, a lad who held the notebook his father had kept in the same course, using the same text by Carpenter, over twenty years earlier, and who, whenever the professor began one of his humorous sallies, would, audible only to those in the rows around him, mouth the very words, jokes and all, his dad had taken down in 1919. Well, chemical engineering, I was sure, was not for me. On the other hand, industrial would be concerned with . . . what? How factories operate? Time and motion studies? In fact I never did have a firm notion of this field's parameters; for the present, I was toiling through the introductory courses all pre-engineers had to take.

The war in Europe seemed far away in 1939–41. Over the radio and in the papers we learned of first the "phony war," then the blitzkrieg. I was in high school, memorizing French irregular verbs, pushing a mower on our suburban lawn the day France fell. In college, studies and campus life were more immediate. Pearl Harbor brought the war closer, but until the draft was instituted it was still a distant thing. The remark of the aged mother of philosophy professor James Gutman was much repeated on campus: hearing on the radio of the Japanese attack that Sunday afternoon, "Formerly," she said, "they would not have interrupted the Philharmonic." As the draft bid fair to depopulate the colleges, the Columbia administration advised enlistment in one or another of the reserve forces. This would allow the students so enrolled to complete their studies before call-up and better prepare them for appointment as officers.

I took the subway downtown to the enlistment office near City Hall. Already, at seven in the morning, there were queues of applicants for the Army, Navy, and Marine Corps. A couple of boys just emerged from the kiosk stood indecisively in the middle of the street, then, seeing that one line was shorter than the others, joined it and so became Marines. I wonder how they fared a year or two later. As for me, I stood behind a score of other young men, mostly college students, in the Army line. Then, assigned a number—12145362—as a private on inactive duty in the Enlisted Reserve Corps, U.S. Army, I took the I.R.T. uptown to Morningside Heights, arriving in time for an economics lecture by Professor Boris Stern. I couldn't grasp much about economics but have never forgotten Stern's reminiscences of having been the administrator of the last city under Menshevik control to surrender to the Bolsheviks in 1921. "To have a revolution," he said, his Russian accent making the words seem portentous and true, "you don't need mass support—just the machinations of a determined minority." But that was ancient history. Now I was a pre-engineer with a chance at a summer job.

Sidney Senzer was willing to look me over, so I went to be interviewed at the Jordanoff Aviation Company. The address, I was surprised to discover, was in a residential neighborhood on the Upper East Side. And it proved to be an apartment house with a uniformed doorman under the marquee. Jordanoff Aviation operated out of an apartment—Mr. Jordanoff's. My ring was answered by a smiling, roly-poly black man, Mr. Jordanoff's butler. In the living room Sidney Senzer rose to greet me. He didn't look well, but then, he never did—pale complexion, moon face, thinning blond hair, and what seemed a vague, shambling air which quite masked his intensity. A long office table was placed incongruously among the couches and armchairs; at it were seated the president of Jordanoff Aviation and a crew-cut Army officer with silver eagles on his epaulets. Sid Senzer took me into an inner room, a bedroom, and sat me down on a stool next to the telephone while he reclined on the bed and asked a few questions. Draft status? He guessed that I, as a college student, had a deferment. Yes, I replied, last year I'd enlisted in the Army Reserve; if I didn't flunk out, I shouldn't be called up until after graduation.

He picked up a folder in pale blue and white, the Columbia colors, and riffled through a few pages. "Good grades in English comp," he said, not mentioning my lackluster technical credentials. "Looks O.K. Can you start tomorrow?" And he sketched my duties, chiefly tagging along with him and "helping." "The job will develop as you do it. We're just getting under way here, so you'll have to be flexible. Our first job is a manual for a fighter plane. I can't tell you anything about it until you've had security clearance."

Security clearance! Secret war work! What luck, what a summer job this would be! The next day I was sent to an F.B.I. office downtown, and within a week Sid was able to reveal our mission: the P-47C, toward which we were speeding on the Long Island Freeway.

★ ★ ★

When he entered a room, he filled it. Big, burly, bronzed, handsome, his very bearing exuded purposeful intensity, a will to dominate and prevail. He combined the assurance of a star athlete with the charm of a European count. Indeed, as I learned over thirty years later reading his obituary, he was the son of a Bulgarian cabinet minister and had been educated in Paris. A pilot from the age of fifteen, he dropped out of school to fly in the Balkan War of 1912. In the First World War he became a much-decorated air ace on the Axis side, scoring, it was said, many kills on the Russian front.

He found postwar Bulgaria too limited an arena for his ambitions and came to the U.S. in 1921 to enter a round-the-world flying race. The announced prize was $100,000, but the competition never got off the ground. He stayed on, first as a stunt pilot, then as an airplane designer and consultant to Curtiss and other aircraft manufacturers. Now he was founder and president of his own firm. Although he'd been in this country for over twenty years, Assen Jordanoff still spoke heavily accented English from which definite article was conspicuously missing.

A few years earlier, having been somehow dragooned to a literary party in New York City, he met Laura Grabbe, a children's book editor at Grossett and Dunlap. Telling this gray-haired woman about himself, Jordanoff entranced her with his vivid descriptions of flying a fighter plane—it's hard now to conceive of the fragility of those World War I crates, canvas biplanes held together with wire struts, the pilot in his open cockpit with a machine gun mounted before his goggled eyes. As Jordanoff, with many gesticulations, enacted piloting in that Manhattan living room, his outstretched hands joined at the thumbs and tilted from side to side as he banked his plane, bending fingers to indicate action of the flaps and ailerons, Mrs. Grabbe, ever the acquisitions editor, exclaimed, You must write a book! A book for boys, a how-to-fly book with lots of illustrations. And so he did. *Your Wings,* with scores of linecuts, appeared in 1935.

This was the time when, Henry Ford having satisfied the American dream of everybody with a Model A in his garage, a new fantasy captured the public imagination: everyone his own pilot, personal monoplane or biplane poised on the driveway. Magazines like *Popular Mechanics* printed plans for building your own aircraft in the backyard. Juan de la Cierva's autogiro was much admired. First flown in Spain in 1923, the craft had a conventional propeller in front but was supported by a rotary wing mounted above the pilot. It was thought that, since it didn't need long runways, this forerunner of the helicopter might become the domestic vehicle of choice. In the event, its reign was brief. Meanwhile, there was a great curiosity, a hunger for aeronautical information. *Your Wings* cleverly pointed at this extant market, as yet served by no other such lively book that made flying seem within everyone's reach. It was a great success.

It must have made Jordanoff a rich man, for there was considerable income, too, from foreign rights. *Your Wings* was adopted by the R.A.F. as a basic training textbook and, in translation, by the Red Air Force as well (no royalties from that edition!). And now this author, who had in fact only a faulty command of English, was moved to supply a new, urgent need in military aviation. By several months after Pearl Harbor it was evident that the U.S. Army Air Corps (Air not yet separated from Army as an independent service, and still a Corps, not yet a Force) had to devise ways to train a civilian population for military duties. This meant that eighteen-year-old kids who had lately been in high school or college, or jerking sodas or pumping gas, would swiftly have to be able to service or fly the most complex aircraft the world had seen. Such technical education required instruction manuals, but what sort of manuals could the Army Air Corps provide for its trainee pilots and flight mechanics?

Supplying an operating manual was required in every procurement contract for military equipment, but few manufacturers had competent technical writers on staff. The task usually fell to the fellow who had nearly flunked out of Rensselaer or Georgia Tech and couldn't be trusted to design any of the actual components. Engineers, as I had observed among my fellow neophytes, were on the whole not especially gifted with verbal facility or writing skills, and the resulting manuals tended to be lists a page or two long of telegraphic directives phrased in engineering jargon. Their nearest equivalents nowadays would be the instructions for VCRs made in Korea. It was to provide readily comprehensible, accurate instruction manuals that Assen Jordanoff founded his company, on the ground floor of which, so to speak, I had joined as his latest and lowliest employee.

★   ★   ★

Acres of cars in the guarded parking lot. Near the sentry box at the gate, a bus stop. Here the security-cleared workers assembled to be taken in groups of thirty or so to the production line inside the hangar maybe half a mile away. And here Sidney and I awaited our in-plant transportation. Once on the bus, we were surrounded by voluble Dodgers, Giants, and Yankees fans, as well as by mechanics discussing the rigors of the work or complaining of an inflexible, time-serving foreman who wouldn't let them off for five minutes for a smoke or a trip to the can. Arriving, we checked in with yet another security officer, then were introduced to a genial guy in coveralls, Mike, the chief flight mechanic, who would be our guide.

Emerging from the security office, we were at the start of the production line. High above us arched the roof of the hangar, which extended ahead for several hundred yards. Here at the beginning, naked airframes like the skeletons of dinosaurs in the Museum of Natural History were on line, and men with riveters and welding torches climbed about them. The skeletons moved down the line, soon becoming carcasses as their interior systems—engine, fuel tanks and lines, electrical components, controls, armaments, etc.—were each added, until, at the end of the quarter-mile progression, completed P-47s rolled off the line on their own landing gear. According to Warren Bodie's detailed history of this plane's development, *Republic's P-47 Thunderbolt: From Seversky to Victory* (Hiawassee, Ga., 1994), the first of fifty-eight P-47Cs was completed on September 14, 1942 (p. 142), so what we were looking at must have been several of the very first planes in production. These were significantly superior to the pioneering design of the P-47B, with improved engine and maneuverability (Bodie, 129); by October further significant changes were made in the plane's rudder, radio, and oxygen system, though of course at the time neither Sidney nor I knew these details. We wrote up the specs for the P-47C as they were given us by the Republic engineers.

With Mike we walked the length of the line as he explained what was going on at each stage. I'd never been close to military aircraft and was astonished by the size of this one. My notions of fighter planes were based on those I'd seen in war movies, 1918 Sopwith Camels, little flying flivvers, or the sleek monoplanes with pants on their wheels flown by Wiley Post in *March of Time* newsreels. But this was a different order of creation.

The P-47C was 35 feet from nose to tail, had a wingspan of 41 feet, and its cockpit canopy was a good 10 feet off the ground. It had an 18-cylinder engine that delivered 2,000 horsepower. It carried eight .50-caliber machine guns, four in each wing, and could bear 3,400 rounds aloft. With fuel tanks filled to 500 gallons, the Thunderbolt had a range of 750 miles (extended in later models to 2,000), could operate at altitudes up to 40,000 feet, and could dive at 500 miles per hour. Its weight, empty of pilot, parachute, fuel, oil, or ammo, was 10,700 lbs; loaded, 3,000 lbs more, the heaviest American fighter. But these figures, taken from the pilot's manual, give scant testimony to the role of this plane in the war. Let me enter here the judgment of W. F. Craven and J. L. Cate, in *The Army Air Force in World War II* (Chicago, 1955):

> The AAF had come by the end of the war to depend still more heavily [than on the P-38] upon Republic's *P-47 Thunderbolt*. In fact after . . . March [1944] inventories never showed less than 5,000 of the planes on hand. . . .
>
> It was a powerful plane. Its engine with more than 2,000 horsepower put the P-47 ahead in this category of all single-engine fighters of the AAF and gave it rank with any other contemporary single-engine fighters in the world.

With its superchargers, the plane climbed fast and performed admirably at high altitude. Its stubby appearance be-
spoke a ruggedness exceeding that of any other AAF
fighter, and no plane of the war proved itself more versa-
tile. (VI, 215–16)

Not until late in the war, when the AAF recognized its need for
long-range fighter escorts for its bombers, was the P-47 equipped
with disposable fuel tanks, but these had to be jettisoned to
maintain maneuverability if attacked by Focke-Wulfs or Messerschmitts. The P-51, with its longer range, displaced the P-47 as
the operational fighter of the Eighth Air Force; P-51s escorted
the B-29s that bombed Japan in 1945 (Craven and Cate,
217–19). The P-47s were assigned to the Ninth Air Force and
attacked preinvasion targets in France and Belgium. The P-47C
was in fact an interim model, of which Republic produced 545;
the 450 sent to Britain from September 1942 to January 1943
were flown by the 4th, 56th, and 78th Fighter Groups. Subsequent models D, M, and N (plus the earlier 170 P-47Bs) brought
the total manufactured to over 15,000 planes (Bodie, 145, 261,
377–79). After the wide introduction of the P-47D, the C model
was used primarily for training pilots—I hope with the Jordanoff
instruction manual in the pockets of their flight jackets.

The P-47C was a huge flying and killing machine, a metallic
metaphor of concentrated purpose. After we'd walked around
the plane a couple of times, Mike brought a ladder up against its
nose, climbed up, took out of his pocket a screwdriver, and gave a
couple of turns to bolts attaching the cowling. He then took
them out, removed a flange of cowling, and came down to show
us. The bolts weren't bolts, they were Dzus fasteners—a new de-
vice, a bolt-head on a short stem with a single slanted slit that
locked the fastener to a staple mounted on the fuselage, thus an-
choring the cowling and requiring only a single turn for removal
or reattachment. "When these babies are on the flight line
between missions," Mike explained, "there won't be time to
screw around with regular threaded bolts—these things are instant openers, instant closers. Seconds count!"

Our rough-drafted notes had to be organized and typed up by

the following Monday morning, so the photographer, arriving then at Farmingdale, would know precisely what to shoot. As Sid lived in Mamaroneck and would spend the weekend with his family (he spent weeknights in Manhattan, at the Peter Stuyvesant Hotel), it was I who would come to work on Saturday morning to revise our notations.

Sid Senzer's special talent was in conceptualizing projects, imagining vivid visual displays, and writing pithy captions. These attributes, so valuable in advertising, he applied now to planning the layout of manuals, organizing step-by-step illustrations and text; pictorial spreads featured warnings and notices. He was the visionary of aeronautical manual-making; his conceptual designs for our first two P-47 projects became the templates for later, larger, more complex Jordanoff manuals, including those completed after Sid had left the company. The format, as I describe it, seems obvious after the fact, but it had not been done before. The field of aeronautical writing and editing was, antebellum, occupied by only a few dozen magazine journalists and publicists for aircraft manufacturers, few if any experienced in preparing instructional manuals.

The format of the instruction book, as Sid designed it, was to resemble a film strip. For instance, the first thing the mechanic had to do to service the plane was to remove the cowling around the engine, so precise instructions on doing this accompanied a series of illustrations of the man inserting his screwdriver into the slot of the first Dzus fastener, removing it, taking out several more, then lifting off the section of cowling so attached. No step was omitted, none elided. There could be no margin for error or misunderstanding in this or in any subsequent, more important act in the required sequence.

Photos of these steps, however, would have been very confusing, for once the cowling was off, a photograph would show a bafflingly intricate forest of flanges, pipes, ducts, plates, piston-heads of the huge engine. The way around that was to have an artist trace in india ink on the enlarged photo only the outline of the engine and those parts to which attention must be given in the step at hand, then reimmerse the print in a defixing solution that washed away the photographic emulsion. What remained was a vivid black-and-white illustration, its details unmistakable, the viewer's attention not distracted by anything extraneous. Accompanying these pictures was the verbal narrative, as concise as possible.

To get our notes into shape for the photographer, I turned up promptly at nine on Saturday morning. I was taken up in the elevator and rang Mr. Jordanoff's bell. A long wait, the door opened, and there stood Assen Jordanoff in his bare feet and blue silk pajamas with embroidered frogs around the buttonholes. "Come in, come in," he said. Behind him the door to the bedroom was still open, so I couldn't help but see a woman still asleep, her long hair falling across the pillow in voluptuous waves. Not in the least embarrassed, Jordanoff motioned me toward a desk in the living room and returned, closing the door behind him. After a time he emerged, dressed, trim, energetic, beaming, followed in a few minutes by his mistress, a tall attractive woman with a way of walking that made it impossible not to notice the proportions of her figure. She, I later learned, was, of course, famous—Jordanoff's woman would have to have been a public figure—as the news commentator on WNYC, the city-owned radio station. She was well known for her liberal, some thought radical, views, which most assuredly the self-made entrepreneur didn't share. But it wasn't her opinions of Soviet Russia that made her interesting to him. They disappeared into the kitchen. The odor of percolating coffee wafted through the flat.

Later that morning, after she had kissed him and gone, the doorbell rang several times. Jordanoff admitted one visitor after another, interviewing them for positions in the new company he had advertised in the paper. By that afternoon the staff had been increased severalfold, perhaps by four or five new members. Overhearing much of what went on, I couldn't help but wonder where they'd all fit into this apartment in which I'd already crowded the boss and his mistress. After the last candidate left and I was folding up my notes, Jordanoff turned to me and said, "Next week, Company move to apartment next door." He had rented the adjacent flat, already furnished with office desks, files, and telephones.

★   ★   ★

Riding the bus from and to the Republic parking lot, Sid and I picked up a lot of information and gossip. The men were certain there had been a compromising intelligence leak concerning a couple of the first planes off the line, which on initial test flights had suddenly spouted plumes of flame and dropped like comets into the Atlantic with the loss of their pilots. It was thought these failures were known to German intelligence, for why else had men from the Secret Service come out to Farmingdale to interview workers and engineers? This was said in undertones; the prevailing theory among our informants was that the site of the leak was the bus. Everyone on it had security clearance, so felt secure in discussing confidential information. But what about the driver? One, called Smitty—what was that, some kraut name, Schmidt? Schmidheiser?—having driven the bus for many months was suddenly seen no more a day or two after the intelligence investigators called in at the plant. Whatever ailed those first P-47s had been fixed long since, and now and again a newly completed plane would roar aloft on its test flight, swooping low over the hangar where it had been born.

The apartment next door proved only a short-term rental. A few weeks later Jordanoff Aviation moved into the top floor of the Fuller Building, an Art Deco office structure many stories tall on the corner of Madison Avenue and 57th Street. By this time Jordanoff had a numerous staff—project directors, writer-editors, draftsmen, artists, and a constant stream of uniformed visitors from the Air Materiel Command at Wright Field in Ohio.

One afternoon Jordanoff called the whole staff together for a meeting. The company, he told us, was about to be awarded several major projects, and it was important we all work well together. Anybody have problem? Everyone satisfied with rate of pay? (No objections heard.) Then we are all set to do really great work and help Air Corps win war.

★   ★   ★

My part in this had quickly grown from carrying Sid's bags to taking notes, to organizing those notes into sections of the manual, to writing the text in those sections. By now, like Sidney and all the other staff members, I had my own desk, and my own notepads with the company logo in the upper-right-hand corner (the initials *AJ*—signifying either "Assen Jordanoff" or "Jordanoff Aviation"—in a blue circle) and, across the top of each page, the legend "From the Desk of Daniel Hoffman." Looking over our notes and my drafted copy, Sid said, "Danny, you can write this as well as I can." We had finished the maintenance manual and were starting the one for the pilots. Partly based on an inadequate set of instructions for the earlier, soon to be replaced P-47B, this book would be similar in format to the one we'd just done. Sid left the completion of this flight manual to me while he went on to plan a much larger, more ambitious project, a maintenance manual for the Boeing B-17 bomber, the Flying Fortress. And so it was that the first book of which I was (virtually) the (anonymous) author was "Published by Authority of The Commanding General, Army Air Forces by The Materiel Command Materiel Center, Wright Field, Dayton, Ohio." A line of very small type at the foot of the title page read "RPX-12 Jordanoff 1-15-43." A 64-page paperback, it was sized to fit in the pocket of the pilot's flight jacket and, I was assured, would have a wide and attentive readership. By then I was nineteen, a college junior who had heretofore published only a few feeble rhymes and sketches in the college humor magazine, *Columbia Jester.*

★　★　★

The process by which photos of each step in the mechanic's examination of the plane were enlarged, the relevant details inked in, then the emulsion removed so that the ultimate illustration was a high-contrast black-and-white drawing, was done by—in fact was said to have been devised by—Jordanoff's art director, Francis Royer. When I joined the firm he, like Sidney, was leader of a one-man band and, also like Sidney, had been in advertising. The initial inking and lab work were done, Sid thought, back at the agency where Royer had been art director, his former associates moonlighting with his new business. And who knew whether they had security clearance? By the time we'd moved into the next-door flat, Royer had an artist or two coming in, and in the Fuller Building his art staff occupied a good part of the floor. Royer was a pencil-thin, tall, darkly handsome man with black sideburns and moustache. He always wore boots and a broad-brimmed hat and looked like a gambler on a Mississippi riverboat. From the Deep South, he held probably well-grounded suspicions of New York, of New Yorkers, and of the New York way of doing business, But, said Sidney, he was a crackerjack art director. The company couldn't have done its work without him.

By summer's end there was a full complement. One project director was Lawson, a ruddy-faced, amiable fellow, middle-aged, in a rumpled suit, given to friendly meaningless greetings before disappearing into an inner cubicle, telephone in hand. After half an hour he'd emerge with the air of one who had just nailed down an essential contract. As perhaps he had done. Another constant telephoner was Roberts, the name given by our White Russian émigré. (Was there ever such a one who hadn't been a count in the old country, or commanded a battalion against the Bolsheviks in 1920?) This intense colleague had a heart condition necessitating constant draughts from a silver-stoppered pocket flask. Just what his function was I never knew. Where Lawson operated on an even keel, Roberts was mercurial; he nearly had apoplexy shouting in his accent into the telephone to a representative of the Bell company—he had to have his apartment phone number changed, from the one he had with zeros and nines, to a number with ones and twos, for both his essential war work and his medical condition required instantaneous connections, not waiting all night for the dial to return from its furthest circumference.

These senior members of the staff and others—Rayburn, McCaffery—were much given, especially when in the presence of lieutenant colonels or majors just flown in from Wright Field, to expatiate on the military philosophy in the much-vaunted book *Victory through Air Power* (New York: Simon and Schuster, 1942) by Major Alexis de Seversky, who had come to this country in 1918 as a member of the Russian Naval Aviation Mission and

16

stayed on after Russia dropped out of the war. His military title derived from his service in the U.S. Specialist Reserve. I wonder how many of those colleagues realized that Seversky was the founder of the firm which, after his being ousted by a stockholders' coup in 1939, became the Republic Aviation Corporation. In the 1930s, Seversky had designed and produced the P-35 and P-43 fighters, forerunners of the P-47, and the innovative design of the P-47's wing, which made it so superior, was his (Bodie, 232). *Victory through Air Power* was a powerful polemic on the need to free air-power administration from its subjection to the Army or Navy. The basic notion of air warfare had been advanced in the twenties by General "Billy" Mitchell and by the Italian general Giulio Douhet, a major though belated influence on wartime American strategic thinking (Stephen L. McFarland and W. P. Newton, *To Command the Sky* [Washington, D.C., 1991], 18–22). Seversky's eloquent book analyzed the battles of the first two years of the war to prove his point. Control of the sea was unavailing to Britain's invasion of Norway without an umbrella of air power, since the crucial Skagerrak Strait was beyond the range of the R.A.F., while the Luftwaffe took off from Denmark and pounded the Royal Navy, vulnerable without air support. And the retreat from Dunkirk was possible because the R.A.F. had temporary local command of the air. Thus Seversky's first examples. He displayed the results of timid and hidebound strategic thinking in the faulty designs of aircraft on both sides: German fighters in 1939–41 had less armament than their World War I counterparts, and their bombers were vulnerable to attack; British Spitfires, on the other hand, were equipped with eight machine guns in the wings. At the start of the war, American fighter planes, designed only to intercept attacks on the continental United States, were slow and had range too limited for optimum use. We were sending disassembled aircraft to England aboard freighters in convoys requiring naval ship and carrier escort, although it was possible to build or equip aircraft for extended flight and self-delivery. Seversky, probably the most experienced aviator-designer and strategist in the United States at the time, proposed to overturn military thinking still based on ground and sea warfare. His proposals for an Air Department independent of both Army and Navy, and for long-range fighters, well-armed bombers, air-cooled radial engines, and tactics based on 15,000-mile range of flight would, if enacted, ensure aerial supremacy. In retrospect these recommendations appear obvious, and in time became policy, but how much sooner would the war have ended had they been in place when it began.

Nonetheless, the subsequent history of World War II and of every war since (except the Gulf War, with its flat terrain and no use of enemy aircraft) has demonstrated the limitations of air power as the single most decisive factor in warfare. The leading historians of the air war preceding the Normandy invasion conclude that

> By the time OVERLORD was sprung, strategic bombing had in and of itself accomplished nothing vital. . . . The missions against aircraft and related production had not yet produced the results claimed at the time. Area bombing had not destroyed morale, much less the infrastructure of the German state. In fact, area bombing seemed to have stiffened the German resolve to keep going.
>
> The major contribution of strategic bombing by June 1944 was its role in bringing about the weakening of the Luftwaffe's fighting arm, particularly the day fighters, through attrition. (McFarland and Newton, 170, 176, 179, 245)

In Korea and Vietnam, far more sophisticated finding and aiming devices were in use than in 1942–45, yet the inaccuracy of high-altitude bombing and its inability completely to stop production and movement of war materiel have been made plain. (To be sure, this knowledge has had little effect on military planning and procurement.) The most recent war, in Kosovo, March–July 1999, gave the theory of victory through air power its most demanding test. Certain that after a few bombing missions against Serbia by the United States and its NATO allies, President Slobodan Milosevic would beg to negotiate a settlement, no one suspected that it would take eleven weeks. Flying at 15,000 feet, committing no ground troops to combat, NATO—principally the U.S.—conducted thousands of missions, destroying much of the Yugoslav infrastructure—bridges, power plants, communications centers—but in no degree halting the Serbian paramilitaries, police, and army regulars from accelerating their campaign of massacres and rapine of the ethnic Albanian Kosovars, the pillage and destruction of their villages, and the forced expulsion of some 800,000 persons, creating a huge refugee problem for neighboring states and for NATO. Not until the Kosovo Liberation Army launched a ground attack, for which NATO had not the will, in sufficient force to bring the Serbian troops and armor out into the open where they could be seen and attacked by NATO aircraft, did Milosevic capitulate. When Kosovo was occupied by NATO forces it became apparent that the claims made of widespread destruction were greatly overstated, many of the targets proving to have been dummies, indistinguishable from the real thing by pilots and bombardiers three miles away in the sky. This experience can stand as proof that the best use of air power is in conjunction with ground attack. Air power alone is a blundering instrument that can neither conquer an enemy army nor prevent its depredations of a civilian population. Victory through air power has long been both a theory and a myth, for believing in it gives the illusion of invincibility without casualties.

When introduced in the Balkan and First World Wars, air warfare consisted of fighter planes fighting each other, such engagements producing our and our enemies' first generation of aviator-heroes like Eddie Rickenbacker, Baron von Richthofen, and, yes, Assen Jordanoff. The main Air Force strategy in Europe in early 1944 assigned to heavy bombers, protected by P-47s and other fighters, the mission previously performed in the dogfights of such pursuit planes: eliminating enemy air power. Among Jordanoff's employees now, this philosophy of victory through air power validated, as an essential part of the war effort, the way they were earning their keep. These were civilians, either overage or deferred for being married or physically 4-F; yet as the war went on, all men not in uniform felt defensive about their civilian status. Believing in the great importance to the war of one's work was a comforting, indeed a much-needed, assuagement of such feelings.

★   ★   ★

Although I didn't even think of it at the time, Jordanoff, with his contacts in the aviation industry and no doubt among venture capitalists eager to invest in a promising business, had, even before landing any major commitments, secured a lot of backing for his fledgling concern. The confidence, energy, and charisma of the man must have been persuasive, although certainly it was also obvious that his planned company would fill an actual need and so would get generous government funding. He must have spent all his time and energy raising funds, securing contracts, negotiating with Air Corps colonels, and arranging the publication of the finished work done by his staff. Although Jordanoff had written several other successful books on aviation after *Your Wings,* as far as I could tell he didn't plan or write any of the manuals. In the few weeks that my presence had been entered as the smallest item on his payroll, Jordanoff's projects were accumulating one after another. Those on which I would work, in addition to the two manuals for the P-47C, were the Sperry A-5 Automatic Pilot and the B-17F bomber.

The company had a treasurer, who was also A.J.'s executive secretary. Was it customary, in the early 1940s, for company treasurers to be women? I don't recall if I ever knew what businesses Serena Stone had managed before joining this one; she exuded an aura of steely competence, was seen at a glance as a no-nonsense sort of person. A glance also showed her to be uncommonly handsome, a tall, sleek woman with raven-black hair, its waves framing her regular, aquiline features, dramatizing the contrast to her perfect white complexion. Her businesslike reserve may well have been, or originated as, a defense against unwanted male attention, of which she must have had more than her share.

We also had an office manager who, in addition to whatever were the duties of that position, did editorial work as well. Freda

Barry, an ebullient, friendly, ash-blonde young woman, could hardly have been more different from Serena Stone yet was her sister. While Serena held herself rather icily aloof from discussing anything save the immediately work-related, Freda loved to schmooze. She soon became the confidante of our messenger girl. Betty was a good-hearted kid just out of high school and came to East 57th Street from her working-class neighborhood in Queens bearing much gossip and many emotional problems involving her classmates and neighbors and complicated strategies involving boys. All were sorted out with Freda's experienced advice. Freda took me up too, and indeed I was buoyed by her friendship in a workplace where I had no other companions. All the other men were middle-aged, each with his own fish to fry and no time for me, a mere kid. Sid was ever amiable, but one's boss is not in the nature of things a pal; besides, he was as old as my father. So I was glad to have Freda's friendship.

She also became the confidante and partisan of Ralph, our security guard, formerly Mr. Jordanoff's butler. He was now stationed near the reception area, the better to check the credentials of all callers as they emerged from the elevators, everyone from Air Corps colonels to delivery boys bringing coffee and sandwiches from a nearby delicatessen. Freda's relationship with Ralph enabled her conspicuously to display her liberal sympathies, chatting and joshing with him on an elaborately equal basis. In the early 1940s black men were not much in evidence in downtown New York except in menial jobs. So Freda made as much as she could of her familiarity with this plump, light-skinned fellow with a high-pitched voice, who modelled himself, at least in his jokey interactions with us white folks, on Fats Waller. That there was anything of a pose in this persona didn't occur to us, any more than Freda could have been aware of her liberal condescension in becoming so determinedly familiar with a man to whom, were he, say, Irish or Italian, she might not have given any particular notice.

Her attitude was a remnant of the Popular Front of her college days. She was, I would guess, in her mid or late twenties (and Serena maybe five to ten years older), so had been on campus when college opinion, formed in the grim Depression, partook of the Popular Front—an enthusiasm to which Serena seemed to have been immune. So Freda favored racial justice, solidarity with the working class and movements on their behalf—the program, in short, of groups like the Young Communist League. This meant, also, enlistment among sympathizers with the Republican forces in the Spanish Civil War. I mention this conflict, concluded seven years before and nearly forgotten in the excitement and anguish of the present war—nightly bombings of London put out of mind the ordeals of Guernica, Barcelona, Madrid—because one day Freda invited me to go with her to a rally that night to raise funds for Republican veterans detained by France in a virtual prison camp. I remember a large, smoke-filled room crowded with young people and few middle-aged enthusiasts passionately singing "Los Quatros Generales" and other anthems of resistance to Franco. The evening's speaker was a veteran of the International Brigade who wore a neck brace as a result, we were told, of a combat injury and spoke haltingly in a heavy German accent about the miserable, doglike existence of the heroes of the siege of Madrid. I had not yet read *Homage to Catalonia* and, in view of our wartime alliance with the Soviet Union, saw nothing inappropriate in this program's concluding with the enthusiastic singing by the audience of "The Internationale," in which, knowing neither the words nor the tune, I haltingly joined.

★   ★   ★

That summer I lived in room 1047, the cubicle I'd occupied all year in John Jay Hall, looking down from my high window on the tennis court, the Van Am Rotunda half-visible through leafy trees in the quiet undergraduate quad, framed on three sides by McKim, Mead and White's high-rise brick dormitories. As summer-school enrollment was down and the Navy V-7 contingent hadn't filled the dorms either, I was permitted to keep my room although not taking courses. This was a boon, since I couldn't live at home in New Rochelle, with my parents in the midst of their acrimonious separation. And besides, I had to be in Manhattan to continue my job, needed not only for the money but to keep me steady with a sense of my own purpose. The room was a hot little box, furnished in spartan style with a deal desk, gooseneck reading lamp, bookcase, one chair, cot, and sink.

This had been my sophomore study hall; here I had struggled to memorize periodic tables, the elements of calculus, the intricacies of free market economies, and, with greater pleasure and success, to comprehend the moral systems and aesthetic philosophies of Plato, Aristotle, and Aquinas and the development of period and individual styles in European music and art since the Renaissance. . . . But now all that was in temporary suspension. Until the start of the fall term, room 1047 was just a place to lay my head.

Classes resumed at the end of September, and I moved to Livingston Hall, in a two-room suite with Stan Goff, an economics major who soon shared my enthusiasm for jazz. We went together to the Village to hear such veteran Chicago jazzmen as Bud Freeman and Muggsy Spanier. It was stimulating to have as a good friend a fellow most of whose interests were entirely different from mine but who was such an enjoyable companion. Across the hall were Sidney Lamb, from Montreal, and Barnett de Jarnett, from Kentucky. These were my special friends. Sid's wry, ironic sense of humor kept us all on balance. Barney, a darkly brooding Appalachian, had about him the air of one who knew himself to be different from the New Yorkers and Easterners around him, one marked for a special destiny. That was to be a poet. He already had a command of technique and a clarity of vision that I could only admire, and more than a little envy. I remember his coming into Stan's and my rooms one night when I was brain-wracked over rhymes that wouldn't come out right; with a quick glance over my shoulder, Barney reached for the pen, crossed out my lame conclusion, and, grasping the thrust of an image that had evaded my labors, wrote in a last line that redeemed the whole effort. How I longed for that instantaneous vision and the language to express it! In November 1942 he wrote out for me a couple of brief poems, one of which appeared in the *Columbia Review* the following spring, by which time we were all elsewhere:

THE SWEET BREATH OF PIPES

The sweet breath of pipes
Warms and mellows the gloom
A Homeric spirit and mine
Inhabit one room.

The carillon plays
A pious devotion to God.
How distant are warriors now,
How cool is my blood.

Tomorrow I clothe
An image in uniform hate
Today there are visions of peace:

Tomorrow, too late.

This little lyric, I see in long retrospect, so much more accomplished than anything I had yet written, rises above the clichés it employs as with admirable compression it evokes the youth studying Humanities A at Columbia and his premonition of going to war. Was I then aware—was Barney?—of the irony in his summoning "A Homeric spirit" to intensify the pastoral image of pipes, Homer offering not bucolics but celebration of a war like that which would overtake us? Barney was, I think, as glad to find a fellow aspirant to the Muse's anvil as was I.

Mornings I attended classes; evenings were for studying and my ear-pulled efforts to write verses. By day, at Jordanoff, I had nearly completed the pilot's P-47C manual and was helping Sid on the B-17F. Next, they'd asked me to study the literature on which to base another set of pilot's instructions, this one for the Sperry A-5 Automatic Pilot. But now I had to go back to college. Sid and the new executive manager of production, George F. McLaughlin, a former *Aero Digest* editor, conferred about the loss of my services, then called me in to propose a solution. "Why don't you work part-time? How about afternoons and Saturdays? You'll have your mornings for classes, your evenings and Sundays for study. We don't want to lose you." My salary would remain unchanged despite the shorter hours. And so in the fall of my junior year I led a double life, after classes bolting a sandwich in the John Jay cafeteria, then rushing downtown and crosstown to the Fuller Building or taking the long subway ride to the Sperry plant in Brooklyn Heights. My economics and philosophy texts were underlined in jerky, wavy lines, replicating the uneven roadbeds of the IRT. Calculus I couldn't study on the subway, nor did I make much progress in it during long nights at the desk.

My life seemed a succession of days in which college prepared me for a life the design of which I couldn't foresee. Commitment to the Industrial Engineering Program pointed to directions less and less appealing. I'd found my fellow pre-engineers not a very stimulating bunch, their intellectual interests confined to the problem-solving exercises of our course work. Evidently their brains and mine had developed differently. A few responded to the elegance they, though never I, perceived in solutions of mathematical quandaries, but the sorts of problems addressed in moral and aesthetic philosophy these fellows found boring. For poetry or literature they had no time at all. I was acting a charade in what others felt to be real life but from which I felt detached, a spectator.

What did give me pleasure was the systematic design of philosophical premises extended through all the facets of experience, the stresses not merely those inherent in strengths of materials or the extended support of weights, but rather such challenges as the nature of virtue and whether identification of the beautiful contributed to the goodness of life. Each author and philosopher read in Humanities A and subsequent philosophy courses proposed a coherent system for interpreting life, a system that contradicted or was contradicted by those of the philosophers and poets read in the preceding as well as the following weeks. These immersions in mutually exclusive explanations of everything excited my imagination and at the same time inoculated me against easy acceptance of any system claiming total validity. The skepticism was stimulating. Among such abstractions I felt more at home than with the solid materialism of civil and industrial engineering problems.

And no class in my scientific-technical courses was as memorable as Mr. Dick's first meeting of English 61, medieval literature. All twenty of us sat silently for forty minutes in a room in which large, mounted prints of Rockwell Kent's dramatic blackand-white illustrations for *Beowulf* were ranged on the chalk shelves of the blackboards, while we listened, on a wind-up portable Victrola, to Howard Hansen's dissonant *Beowulf Suite*. That was it—then go read the poem and come in Wednesday prepared to discuss it. And at the end of this course I got up my nerve to turn in as a term paper my own fabliaux in what I hoped were Chaucerian couplets. The plot involved my roommate Stan Goff and me in a bit of sophomoric high-jinx. No sooner had I left it in Mr. Dick's mailbox in Hamilton Hall than I was seized with self-condemnation for my folly, but Mr. Dick seemed to appreciate, if not the belabored jest, at least the efforts at rhymed metrical composition. He took an interest in my progress, and when I was called up for active service gave me a Daumier print of an elderly man, more than a little resembling Henry K. Dick, raising his tricorne to a young cadet standing at attention (this must have alluded to the Franco-Prussian War of 1870–71). It was titled *Jeune et vielle garde*. The cadet looked a little like Private Hoffman. We corresponded during the war; Mr. Dick's letters about his life in the trenches in France twenty-five years earlier made a contrast to my stateside duty.

Writing poems, or at any rate verses, in time stolen from my studies and my job became a private indulgence, a source of both frustration and pleasure unlike any other. I was encouraged by Mr. Dick's interest in my writing, which he held to standards far more demanding than those I had yet internalized.

★　★　★

At Jordanoff, the company was spread out among many projects. Tevis Rayburn, a former pilot, and Jack McCaffery were sent out to the West Coast, each to start a new manual under Sid's direction. I was left on my own without my mentor, riding the I.R.T. to the Sperry factory in Brooklyn. A month or so later, the West Coast contingent were having difficulties, a problem discussed in a meeting by McLaughlin, Serena, Freda, Royer, and a new vice president, Mr. Taylor. After Francis Royer pointed out that I was the only one on the force besides Sid who had actual experience in manual writing, they asked wouldn't I go out to the Coast and help McCaffery. From this I inferred that my P-47 flight manual had been adjudged O.K. But, I told them, if I dropped out of college I'd be called immediately to active duty and so wouldn't be able to do anything for the laggard manual in California.

A few weeks into fall term I got a note from Dean Hawkes calling me in for a talk.

"You wished to see me, sir?" I asked. Of course he wished to see me, that's why he'd summoned me to his office. The dean was a rotund man with a moustache who looked as though a Toby jug had come to life. An experienced administrator of Columbia College, he had heard every conceivable cockamamie story from erring students.

"Hoffman," he said, "I've been looking at your record, and have to conclude that you are the only man in the one-hundred-and-eighty-seven-year history of Columbia College who has ever taken calculus four times and neither passed nor failed." I explained how I'd dropped it the first time because ill, had taken it again and passed the quizzes but failed the exam, then had been permitted to enroll in differential on condition that I repeat the integral course yet again. Now I was struggling through both at once. "That explains part of your problem," he said, "but you are now carrying only three courses instead of the required four."

"Well, I had to drop economics this term so I'd have enough time to study math. Economics is a sort of math too, and I couldn't handle it all."

"Why don't you get a tutor in economics? Don't you realize that with less than a full load you are going to be called up by the Enlisted Reserve?" I thanked the dean for his suggestion but said I was working twenty-six hours a week, from one to five every weekday and on Saturdays from nine to three, writing Air Corps instruction manuals at the Jordanoff Company, and so had no time either for a tutor or for further study of economics.

"I had no idea of what you are doing. No doubt the work you describe may be more important to the war effort than whatever assignment you are likely to get in uniform, but you must understand that I have no choice in the matter. The college must abide by the government's regulations. Perhaps you can persuade the Reserve Board to let you finish both your work and your studies, but Columbia cannot undertake to do that."

Reporting this conversation to Mr. Jordanoff and Serena led to my immediate promotion. Although neither my duties nor my salary—twenty-five dollars a week—was changed, I was now to be identified as "assistant editor." They thought that a title of such gravity might help defer my call to active duty. Serena asked to see the letter I'd write to the Reserve Board, and she gave me the names of the company's attorneys in case verification of my employment was required.

By now I had concluded that my work at Jordanoff was engineering enough for me. Without further intellectual self-abasement or humiliation, I could understand and clearly describe the way a plane flew, the things that had to be done to keep it safely aloft, and how to operate its autopilot. Now I was determined to get out of the engineering curriculum. To do this I had to get the permission of the adviser to pre-engineers, J. Dexter Hinckley, Associate Dean of the Engineering School. His secretary told me I could find him in the parking lot beside the Chandler Chemistry Building. So there I went, and there, in the barricaded lot from which cars were barred, was Mr. Hinckley in an asbestos suit with a huge helmet and unwieldy gloves, holding a flaming acetylene torch against a metal something that glowed white-hot, testing whatever it was for some Army specification. It took several minutes for him to become aware of my presence. He shut the flame down to a blue bud, lifted the visor of his helmet, and turned to me.

"Mr. Hinckley, I've come to tell you I want to switch from pre-engineering to major in philosophy."

"Good," he said, dropped his visor, turned up the torch, and resumed his high-temperature test.

★   ★   ★

Losing myself in course work and in Jordanoff assignments was a welcome alternative to the chaos of my family life. I'd been going home weekends to scenes of bitter recriminations. A divorce, of course, would have made a clean ending to the dilemma of two such incompatible persons as my parents being yoked together. But the laws of New York State at this time, under the influence of a heavily Roman Catholic legislature, allowed only one ground for dissolving a marriage. And neither my father nor my mother was willing to undergo the humiliating charade of arranging, through a lawyer's connivance, the overnight stay in a hotel with hired consort, photographer, and witnesses. Instead, after exchanges of charges and countercharges in blue-bound sheafs from the offices of legal firms with several names on their letterheads, they achieved legal separation—this was during my sophomore year—each living for the nonce in a rented room in some stranger's apartment. The house in New Rochelle was let; my sister Vivian, in high school, lived with our aunt, my mother's sister, a physician, her engineer husband (in whose plant I had helped make air-conditioning ducts the previous summer), and their young daughter.

On what must have been my last weekend in New Rochelle, the Saturday morning was spent driving to the local bank in whose basement were placed for safekeeping all the silver and other valuables from our disintegrating household. Here I served as witness to the division of these spoils of my parents' twenty-year marriage as, checking a lengthy detailed inventory in my father's hand, a bank clerk divided into equal moieties the pairs of pheasant-shaped silver pepper shakers, sets of coffee spoons, silver plates, goblets, napkin rings to be stored henceforth under their separate names. I have had since, and am sure I had at the time, the simultaneous sense of being present and of witnessing the scene as though I were elsewhere looking on. Seeing these familiar furnishings of home and childhood wrapped, boxed, labelled, and stored like so much merchandise in a warehouse did little to give me a sense of anything to come home to.

How curious, how ironic, that of all the quondam students in Math 32 or drafting, I was the one gainfully employed in the work of real engineers. My classmates had most of them spent the summer prolonging childhood as counsellors at camps or doing odd jobs or driving ice-cream trucks in the suburbs, but here was I involved in really challenging work, on which what skills I had in analytical thinking and writing clear prose were being put to significant uses. Besides, I felt I belonged to a community, the staff at Jordanoff. All were of one mind, worked well with one another, took pride in the success of our company as one project after another was completed to the praises of Major Baldwin and the other officers who worked with us, and their superiors at Wright Field. From Betty the messenger girl to Sid, Royer, Lawson, and McCaffery to McLaughlin and Jordanoff himself, we all had *esprit de corps.*

So I took real satisfaction in doing a war job with real responsibilities. The instructions in our manuals had to be absolutely accurate, all steps in the right order, nothing omitted, all phrased so clearly that any reader could enact the directions without error. I'd always wanted to write—had even taken an extension writing course at Columbia which, disappointingly, taught merely how hacks survey the market and submit outlines of salable articles to editors of trade magazines or community newspapers. Not what I had in mind at all. I was struggling to write poems, a form for which no writing course was offered, poems in outworn conventions based on my reading of anthology chestnuts, since I was completely unaware of contemporary literature. Expressing feelings, ideas, truths, processes in language, with all its equivocal possibilities, its metaphoric power and the allurements of its sounds, the rhythms of syntax—all this was deeply appealing to me. But poetry was a private pleasure. What I might write on my own was still in the future; meanwhile, this employment gave me a sense of professionalism, an identity, and, as I was told my work was well done, pride and self-confidence, both sorely needed.

★　★　★

Having left the P-47C pilot's manual to me, Sid now could give his undivided attention to a much more ambitious project: the maintenance manual for the B-17F. When I'd completed my own project and helped with the A-5 Automatic Pilot book, I was reassigned to Sid, so had a small part in the writing. If the P-47 was the world's largest fighter plane, the B-17 Flying Fortress was the biggest bomber. Each was a huge, complex creation, in the maintenance of which every system required the most scrupulous attention. Here again the personnel involved would be young men who in civilian life a few months before might not even have tinkered with cars, yet who, after being quickly shoved through mechanics' school, had the care of the B-17 thrust upon them. The problem, as always in military technical instruction, was how to make easily accessible and unambiguous the procedures—the sequences of inspections and, when needed, corrections of detected flaws—absolutely required for the safe operation of the aircraft.

We had to consider the number of complex systems aboard, any and all of which could be subject to the deteriorations of normal use as well as being vulnerable to enemy fire or accidents. There was, for starters, the metal skin enclosing the airframe and its constituent parts—fuselage, wings, flaps, ailerons, tail, rudder, engine housings, propellers, landing gear. There was the fuel system: fuel tanks sufficient for extended flight, with their controlled feeder lines into the four engines. A hydraulic system raised and lowered the landing gear, directed the armaments, operated the directional components. The electrical system controlled the hydraulics, as well as instrumentation, power plants, radio, bombsights, etc. Each of these systems was a network of interrelated parts and functions, the circuits of wires, pipes, mechanical controls mostly hidden from sight. How to instruct the G.I. at maintenance school so that he would understand the complexity of this gigantic machine, know where to find what he needed to inspect, and what to do when he found it?

Sid, in charge at the inception of this work, conceptualized the manual's divisions to correspond to the systems to be successively inspected, and drafted the outline of the whole shebang. But the illustrative material had to be more complex than the inked-over photos we had used for the fighter plane. One proposed solution, to illustrate the engine, must have resulted from some executive-level negotiations between Jordanoff and another concern. The proposal was to adopt to the needs of this guide a form of visualization developed for medical textbooks. Transparent plastic pages, overlaid precisely one on another, comprised a visual aid in which the medical student, opening his text to the illustration, looked at a naked human body. Turning the first transparent page, he had removed its skin and was now able to study the vividly multicolored circulatory system—the veins, the arteries, and heart came in plain view. Another page revealed the musculature of the patient; turn that, and the nervous system appeared, and so on until, finally, the skeletal structure was seen.

This technique had been produced by the Millprint Company of Minneapolis, who became associated with Jordanoff in the B-17 project. In the manual, published as *Familiarization and Inspection Manual for the B-17F Flying Fortress,* the opening section was headed "Trans-Vision of the Power Plant / Wright Cyclone 9 Cylinder Engine," model R-1820. There were four such engines to power the Fortress. The "transvision" presented twelve pages, each printed on both sides, so that as the pages were turned the images were subtracted from the right-hand pages but other views were superimposed on one another on the left-hand pages, giving a complete visual presentation of every part of the complex engine. As a lowly subeditor, I knew not how or by whom this joining of the editorial and printing companies had been effected or what were the contractual arrangements. All I knew was what was required of me and what the design of the finished manual was meant to be. The success of this visual aid required the greatest exactitude in printing the transparent pages. Their binding allowed no tolerance of variation, they must be superimposed with precision. This process was of course very expensive.

The rest of the 510-page manual proceeded differently. The individual systems each were described and illustrated with fold-out double pages in color. The latter half of the tome was devoted to inspection procedures. After a series of charts outlining procedures for pre-flight, after-flight, daily, 25-, 50-, and 100-hour inspections, there followed, on pp. 278–494, step-by-step illustrations like those for the P-47C maintenance manual. These covered inspections of the aircraft and, in a separate section, of the armaments.

I was called to active duty before this project was finished, but while in the service got hold of a copy. By this time Sid Senzer had been forced out of the Jordanoff Company, his work appropriated and completed—and credit for it claimed—by others.

By the time I left, in January 1943, the Jordanoff staff had grown still further, and as it grew its character changed. Where the original appointees, Sid and Francis Royer, were masters of their respective crafts, indeed had the personalities of artists *manqués,* the new, higher-level appointees came from different backgrounds. They were competitive business types and engaged in intrigues of Machiavellian complexity in their efforts to be assigned the largest and most lucrative contracts. For this kind of maneuvering Sid had neither the temperament nor the stamina. For all of his talent, Sid lacked decisiveness and could not survive long in such a nest of plots and betrayals.

When completed for our biggest bomber this was the biggest maintenance manual ever seen, as thick as a Manhattan telephone directory, larger, heavier. Hard to visualize this unwieldy tome with its fine-tuned color plates having its pages flipped by greasy fingers on the flight line. It was destined to be studied apart from the hurly-burly pace of actual flight inspections between missions, to be memorized by crew chiefs for future use. This encyclopedic and gargantuan volume could not be carried around, had to be laid out on a desk or table. It was in fact not an operational manual but a work of reference.

How many thousands of dollars each copy cost the government or how many copies were actually produced, distributed, and used to maintain B-17Fs in action, I have no way to know. This must have been a very expensive project in every aspect of its production save the salaries of its editors. A year or so later, when in the Air Force, I got a letter from Freda Barry telling me that the Jordanoff Company hadn't been paid for this work after all; there was a claim against Millprint for infringement of another company's patents. How this contretemps was resolved, if ever it was, I never found out. While in the service I saw another Jordanoff manual, which must have been prepared after I left the company—a similarly elephantine tome for the C-54A cargo plane, with exactly the same layout and organization: a set of plasticene transparencies dissecting its engine (the Pratt and

Whitney Twin Wasp 14-cylinder model R-2000-7), again followed by fold-out double-page color illustrations of its constituent systems, with charts and step-by-step depictions for inspection.

After the war I learned that on May 3, 1943 (by then I'd been in the Army since March), the Jordanoff Aviation Company reformulated itself as the Jordanoff Aviation Corporation, with George F. McLaughlin as vice president and Serena Stone as secretary and treasurer. But two weeks later, Harold G. Fitzpatrick, an attorney and the company's controller, replaced Serena. She had been Assen Jordanoff's executive secretary from the moment the company was formed but was now summarily dismissed. And, as the *New York Times* reported on September 2, "Thomas H. Corpe has been made vice president and general manager of the Jordanoff Aviation Corporation." By this time Sid Senzer had been forced out and had gone back to an advertising agency, and as Freda wrote me—she too was gone by then—Corpe had eliminated just about all of the original staff from the payroll. Serena founded a rival company, Techtronics, enlisting Freda and several other Jordanoff alumni. Francis Royer, similarly squeezed out, also started a rival firm of his own. The *esprit de corps* of a year earlier had quite vanished with all these defections and forced ousters, as the management—Corpe, and no doubt Jordanoff himself—pursued growth of the corporation as their primary goal.

What had begun as a bright idea to fill a perceived need, creatively solving instructional problems for the Army Air Corps, had become an ever-expanding entity with an impersonal existence of its own, staffed by veterans of the competitive wars in other fields of business. The Jordanoff Corporation soon became too big for its own independent survival. Its successes made it a target for acquisition by an older, larger, more opulently financed concern. At some time in 1944—the *Times* does not record this transaction—the Jordanoff Corporation was swallowed up by Lockheed. This firm before the war produced only civilian aircraft, but its twin-hulled fighter, the P-38, launched it as a major producer of military aircraft (and later, of spacecraft). In the Lockheed empire, absorption of the Jordanoff manual unit must have provided no more than a footnote in the corporation's annual report. (Over fifty years later, neither Lockheed nor a search of libraries could supply that corporation's report for 1944.)

The Jordanoff firm had ceased to exist, and there are no further entries under that name in the index to the *New York Times* until Assen Jordanoff's obituary on October 19, 1967. This career summary was headed "AVIATION PIONEER / Stunt Flier is Dead at 71—Fought in World War I" but failed to identify him as one of a handful of the very first military aviators, having flown in the Balkan War of 1911–12. While describing the success of his books on aviation ("He contended that much time in instruction could be saved by illustrated, textual lessons") the obituary says, rather mysteriously, of the context in which I knew this remarkable man, "During the war [he] started the Jordanoff Aviation Corporation, which engaged in research projects." Of the subsequent fate of Jordanoff Aviation, or of A.J.'s postwar career, nothing is said. From this death notice I learned that before forming his company he had been married to a granddaughter of President Grant.

★   ★   ★

Word of my impending call-up to active duty spread around the office. Several officers from Wright Field were frequently there to oversee manuals in production and advise on which equipment Jordanoff should submit proposals for new ones. A captain who had followed with particular interest the work on the fighter manuals suggested that I see Colonel Hodge in New York: "He represents the Eastern Procurement District of the Materiel Command. Tell him what you've been doing here, and see what he says." So I made an appointment. In a few weeks I received a letter headed

Address reply to
Commanding Officer
HEADQUARTERS
WRIGHT FIELD
Office of the Commanding Officer

JJB/jjd/10
Dayton, Ohio
Feb. 24, 1943

Mr. David G. Hoffman
434 Livingston Hall
Columbia University
New York, N.Y.

Dear Sir:

Communication has been received to the effect that you are to be inducted into the armed forces in the near future and that you desire to work in the Technical Data Office of this station. Your qualifications and past experience have been reviewed and we feel that your services can be utilized to a definite advantage in our office.

It is requested that you wire this Headquarters your Army Serial number, organization and station, reception center and date of induction immediately after your induction to enable this office to request your transfer while you are still in the reception center.

Yours very truly,
JOHN J. BISHOP
Captain, Air Corps
Personnel Officer

Even though addressed to "David" G. Hoffman, this letter gave a sense of solidity to my forthcoming change of role. It was settled. What the Technical Data Office was or did I didn't yet know, but that was where my "services" could be "utilized to a definite advantage." While at the reception center I would be summoned from Dayton and would immediately proceed to Wright Field to have my services utilized forthwith.

My employment at Jordanoff came to its close just before final exams at the end of January. I had to vacate my dorm room, so packed my books in cartons, clothes in a suitcase, and in my father's car took these and my old Remington standard typewriter to my aunt and uncle's house in New Rochelle for storage in their basement until after the war. I'd stay with them, bunking on their sleeping porch, until reporting for duty. The call from the War Department arrived to report to Camp Upton on March 3. Both my parents came together at Penn Station to see me off on the Long Island train, and made me promise to write often.

The *New York Times* I read on the train reported "CENTER OF BERLIN BLASTED IN HEAVIEST RAID"—the R.A.F. had dropped 900 tons of bombs on the smoking city—and "AMERICANS PUSH FARTHER INTO TUNISIA," retaking Sbeitla, from which our troops earlier had been driven. And King George V had taken a job in a munitions factory two days a week. Looked like this war couldn't last much longer.

II

A motley crew we were, wearing civvies for the last time as we shivered in a wavering line outside a Quonset hut. One by one we were admitted to have our dog tags cut and given us, then on to another line at another temporary building for the issuance of boots and uniforms. When at last my turn came, I stepped toward a counter behind which a G.I. pounded the keyboard of a machine that mated an oversized typewriter with a metal punch. Each of us carried a card on which was written our serial number—mine was 12145362—and blood type.

I handed the card to . . . he *did* look familiar . . . it took me a couple of minutes to realize that the woebegone youth in winter khakis and crew-cut manning the keyboard was the author of last year's Varsity Show on Morningside Heights—Izzy Diamond, later renowned as I. A. L. Diamond, collaborator with Billy Rose and writer of many a Hollywood screenplay. "Izzy, is that you?" "Alas yes," he replied. "Listen, don't tell them you've been to college," he advised. "If you say that, they'll know you can type."

At Classification, I suppressed my collegiate experience, saying merely that I'd prepared aviation manuals. Thus I was spared assignment as clerk-typist and was set down instead as Technical Information Specialist. That night I wired Captain Bishop my new serial number and whereabouts, as his letter directed, and confidently waited for orders to go to Wright Field. Several days passed—K.P. duty, fumbling introductions to close-order drill in the bitterly cold winter wind, poker games in the tent, the same guys winning all the time, getting rich. Each morning, in the predawn darkness at lineup, the sergeant barked out the names of those to be shipped out to basic training.

During this first week at Upton there was a casualty. A new recruit was assigned to man a bulldozer—we heard he came from a farm somewhere upstate—and enlarge the parade ground, pushing load after load of cleared brush and earth to make a mound at the field's edge. Somehow, climbing this mound, his machine tipped over and he was crushed. Turned out he wasn't an experienced tractor driver. He'd been a clerk in a shoe store.

After several days, while I waited for a response from Captain Bishop—had none come because I'd signed the telegram "Daniel," not "David," as his letter was addressed?—I was dismayed to hear the sergeant call, among the names for that day's shipping list, mine. Within an hour, G.I kit slung over my shoulder, I was part of a weary line boarding a slow train to Florida for eight weeks of basic training, and then assignment—to what I was no longer sure.

★ ★ ★

The troop train took three days. Chugging through Maryland, we passed the hangars of the Martin Marietta plant and saw camouflaged bombers. For the rest of the journey we were frequently pulled over onto sidings in the woods and barrens, the only signs of life curls of bluish smoke rising from an occasional ramshackle wooden or tar-papered cabin, some with tin roofs gleaming in the sun, while endless freight trains chugged past, staining the sky with their smoke. These were carrying essential materials for war production, while our aged cars, furnished with stained, faded, worn plush seats, had a cargo only of untrained soldiers-to-be. I'd never been farther south than Washington, so the landscape—the woods, mountains, deserted streams, poverty-stricken villages along the tracks, occasional small cities with factories bordering the rivers—all this was novel. So, as we inched southward, was the heat in the cars, airless even with all windows opened.

At last, arrival in Miami, then bussed to our destination— Miami Beach. A scruffy, unkempt lot of buck privates were we who fell out and lined up in a parking lot, collected our gear, and then were marched, as best we could, to our quarters. My digs and those of several dozen others were in the Indian Creek Hotel, a recently built Art Deco apartment-hotel across the street from the creek—a canal inlet from the ocean—which ran parallel to the beach a couple of blocks away. Oceanside were high-rise hotels, the expensive tourist resorts, some requisitioned by the Army. No doubt the trainees billeted in these had better views than we did, but all must have been as crowded as the troops in the Indian Creek. I shared a bridal suite of two small rooms with eight others.

We had arrived the week after two German spies rowed ashore from a submarine in an inflatable raft. They were immediately captured, but this invasion of a fifteen-mile coastal resort by a landing party of two had the whole place in a paroxysm of excitement and concern. The civilian vacationers were said to be frightened, threatening to desert the endangered resort. Military precautions were ordered effective immediately—double guard patrols at night and, at sea, intensive searching by boat and aircraft for the enemy sub. This mini-invasion gave our drill instructors all the impetus they needed to turn us greenhorns into seasoned troops ASAP, at least as far as close-order drill and calisthenics were concerned.

The regimen of physical training and intensive instruction, sessions at the rifle range, endless drill in the dust and heat, parades, was all exhausting for men who had been indolent civilians only weeks before. Hot and tiring though it was, I most enjoyed drill and parade formations. Our drill instructor, a virtuoso, taught us intricate maneuvers so that our performances were pleasing to those doing them. Close-order drill, intended to make men instantly responsive to commands, also works to weld them together through their being parts of maneuvers in unison, a physical bonding at the same time partaking of the primitive elements of rhythm and something akin to dance. At parades we had a first-rate marching band to set the swinging tempo with Sousa marches, "High Society," and other rousing tunes whose titles I never learned. Nights, we sacked out, incongruously swathed in the opulent fragrance of the jasmine blooming in profusion below our windows.

After eight weeks we had shaped up pretty well, except for one guy in my suite who'd been drafted from his college studies in physical education. Basic training ought to have been his element, but either he was away from home for the first time and missed his mommy or he was so frightened of the possibilities of his next assignment that he cracked up, rising from blubbering nightmares in a trance to do sit-ups and push-ups noisily in the middle of the night. Finally he was removed from our company, and at last the rest of us could sleep until the too-early reveille brought us tumbling into the street for roll call.

Basic training ended, we awaited orders. Several days went by; men were shipped out, a score or a dozen at a time, to gunnery or radio school or other, undesignated assignments. Where would I go? I had with me Captain Bishop's letter and showed it to the company commander, a lieutenant promoted from the ranks in the prewar regular Army. "This Bishop must be one of your direct-commission captains," he said. "Doesn't know there's no such thing as a G.I. without basic training. And who ever heard of a B.T. unit at a Command HQ!" "Sir, do you think an order for me is working its way through Army red tape?" "Don't bet on it," he counselled. "Looks like they want you at Wright Field, though, so you'd better send your captain another wire. Tell him you're a soldier now."

After several further days the orders arrived at last. I entrained again, this time for Dayton, Ohio.

★   ★   ★

My orders were, report to Commanding Officer, Technical Information Section, Technical Data Laboratory, HQ Materiel Command, Wright Field. From the Dayton train depot an Army bus took me and handful of other enlisted men on the ten-mile trip through villages and farms to the sprawling base at Wright Field, a city of two- and three-story buildings spread out on a hillside, at the bottom of which were several hangars and an airfield. Several planes, DC-7s, a B-26, a B-17, and a couple I'd never seen before, one with British markings, stretched their wings on the runways. My destination, I was told by the guard at the gatehouse, was the Aeronautical Library Building, near the bottom of the hill. This was an Art Deco structure housing a large reading room and, upstairs, several chambers and offices. As I took the directed path to the C.O.'s office I walked through a long hall of desks at which men, both officers and civilians, intently studied bound sheafs of specifications, blueprints, and other documents. One earnest, bespectacled civilian in a gray suit had a metal dish two feet in diameter on his desk, and into this fed page after page of a document, watching each be consumed by flame: the contract specifications, I later learned, for an experimental fighter already obsolete, still secret though abandoned and never to be put in production. Perhaps it was the Republic P-41.

After reporting to Colonel J. M. Hayward, chief of the Tech Data Lab, I was sent to see Captain Henry Ross, a rotund, amiable man who had made motion pictures before the war and was in charge of the Technical Information Section. His deputy, Captain Doy L. Hancock, had a bronzed complexion, a firm handshake, and genially welcomed me. Among the units in the Technical Data Laboratory were a photographic section that made training films; an art section where illustrations, diagrams, posters, visual aids of all sorts were designed and executed; a manuals and a translation unit; and an editorial section where a magazine, *The Technical Data Digest,* was produced. This is where I was assigned.

And what was *The Technical Data Digest*? It was described, in official memoranda, as "Official Journal of the Army Air Corps

Research & Development Program." In fact it published no original research; it was a 32-page collection of abstracts of articles
from current aeronautical journals. I was told by Miss Eileen
Leane, the dedicated, bespectacled, middle-aged civil servant in
charge, that it had begun before the war—as far back as in
1930—as an information sheet circulated to engineers and other
staff at each of the laboratories on Wright Field: Aircraft Design,
Armament, Aero Medicine, Personal Equipment, Power Plant,
Photographic, Propeller, Materials. In addition to these cate-
gories, abstracts were made of the latest publications on fuel,
radio, and aircraft production. The brief summaries were to keep
up to date the personnel working on projects at these laboratories, and to refer them to articles they could read in full, if they
felt the need, in the Aeronautical Library. But after Pearl Harbor
there was a sudden demand for this information elsewhere,
among Air Corps personnel at other bases and among engineers
at firms producing military equipment.

"I'm a bit confused," I said. "My experience is in preparing instruction manuals—I thought that's what I was sent here to do."

"Well, from time to time we may be asked to help with a
manual, but your job," Miss Leane told me, "is, first, to read several issues to get an idea of what an abstract is, then to write up
the articles that look important, in no more than three hundred
words," from magazines on a list she would give me. She,
Sergeant Braxton, a secretary, and I were the entire staff of this
digest. Looked as though I was on the ground floor of another
aeronautical publishing venture.

Sergeant Braxton was the type who knows he's a candidate for
Greek god at an interfraternity ball. He wore a pair of wings on
his chest and said he'd been through bombardier school, but that
on being tested again after graduation, his eyesight didn't meet
required specs. He'd written advertising for the Piper Company,
so ended up here.

This seemed rather an amateurish team to be condensing
technical literature—a woman civil servant, formerly a librarian,
without technical background, and this smooth sergeant who
also lacked relevant credentials. The abstracting of material from

Aero Digest, Journal of Aeronautical Engineering, and all the relevant trade journals and publications of engineering societies, and similar British and Canadian literature, required not that one could follow the theoretical presentations or comprehend the mathematical equations often crucial to their argument, but be able to summarize the prose sense of the argument so clearly that an engineer, a crew chief, a technician or civilian scientist working on Air Corps projects could understand its gist and tell whether he needed the abstracted article. The ideal abstract would so well condense the meaning of that article that a reader remote from the Wright Field Library wouldn't need to consult it.

For much of the first month or so I felt out of my depth. Gradually I got the hang of how to do this job, how recognize which equations were essential to the thesis and so include them in the abstract, and how summarize as tersely but accurately as possible the contribution of each article. In a year's time I had condensed several hundred technical articles on all sorts of subjects; for example, from one of the first issues (August 1943) to which I contributed and in which I'd marked my own abstracts, there were, *inter alia,* "Aerodynamic Performance of the Towed Glider" (from *Journal of Aeronautical Sciences*), "Pressurizing Low-Altitude Airplanes" (*Aero Digest*), "Detectives of Flutter" (*Canadian Aviation*)—and here was one in which I was particularly interested, from the British journal *Flying:* "First Analysis of the Thunderbolt." Other titles I abstracted include "Enemy Weapons" (*Army Ordnance*); from *Automobile Engineer* an article, "Creep Strength: Its Relation to Fatigue Strength," translated from a German source; "Finishes for Plywood in the Aircraft Industry" (*Mechanical Engineering*); and another I read with particular attention, "Boeing, Douglas and Vega Build the Flying Fortress," in *Aviation* magazine. Regardless of my inability to pass differential calculus, I was getting an education in engineering.

The abstracts, arranged under topical headings, were copied by the *Digest*'s secretary, Jennie McDaniel, on a varityper. Until just before my arrival the *Digest* had been mimeographed, so varityping was seen as an improvement. This contraption had an oversized typewriter keyboard and automatically justified the typed copy so that the right-hand margin was regular. The only drawback was the typeface, a semibold, ugly font, uninviting to the eye, as the letters were jammed together in some lines or stretched out with space between them in others, to keep the right margin flush. The result was inelegant copy; the advantage, this was a lot cheaper than hot or cold type. Column after column of abstracts came out of the varitype's roller; these we cut to page-length size and pasted up on dummies, to be photographed for offset reproduction at the in-house printing plant near the flight line. Even with the photostat of an occasional diagram or illustration inserted in the columns, the makeup was about as lively as that of a telephone directory.

I had arrived just fourteen months after Pearl Harbor, and it was apparent that Materiel Command Headquarters still had the outlook of the prewar Air Corps, although changing daily into an organization better able to handle the tremendous demands for new designs of equipment, vast expansion of procurement, influxes of added personnel. All these changes altered the character of the base. The prewar Air Corps, like the Army of which it was a part, was a small-scale outfit, underfunded, undermanned, set in its ways, handicapped by both scant Depression financing and the isolationism of the American people and their Congress. The sorry state of the American aircraft industry just before the war in Europe began is revealed in Warren Bodie's history of the development of the P-47:

> No more than 36,000 people in every job level were employed by the combined aircraft and engine industries in 1938. Industrial assets came to an appalling total of only $125 million. That was a *combined total* for all aircraft and engine builders in the 48 states!
>
> One major brewery or motion picture studio at that time could boast of greater net worth than two combined industries whose disappearance could precipitate world domination by one man. (*Republic's P-47 Thunderbolt,* 103)

On the military side of our unpreparedness, isolationism decreed a "Fortress America" attitude. What development was permitted of fighter aircraft was limited to those designed to intercept enemy bombers attacking our shores. Support for long-range bombers and fighters able to escort them 1,000 miles from base had to wait until after our entry into the war. At first the best we could do was adapt existing models.

Perhaps the deployment of planes at Pearl Harbor, even after intelligence of possible attack, lined up in rows like privates at attention, easy targets for the Zeroes that blew them to smithereens, symbolized the rigidity and lack of imagination that all too often characterized the services in the 1930s. This was the Air Corps in which General Billy Mitchell's predictive tactics had been derided and ignored. In the cubicle of the Technical Information Section, the abstracting function, which could have been organized and operated by scientifically trained personnel, was the routine duty of the woman in charge. An admirable civil servant, Miss Leane, a former librarian, did the best she could despite her lack of technical education and the scant resources available to her. The sudden expansion of the magazine's readership surprised everyone connected with it.

★   ★   ★

There were, from time to time, changes at the very top. We'd get a new Commanding General, not that we worker ants had any direct contact with whoever wore the stars and was driven around in a khaki limousine with a flag on its fender. One such change of command, however, did bid fair to affect us all. General William S. Knudson, lately the C.E.O. of General Motors, then Director of Production for the War Department, on arrival in August 1944 decided that he would operate Wright Field the way he had run his company, now so deeply involved in war production. All this military nonsense that got in the way of the real work to be done, this would have to go. For starters, he would not be known as Commanding General; all ukases emanating from his office would be signed "By Order of the Director."

This was to be the first of many measures demilitarizing Wright Field, but it met with considerable resistance. Even— perhaps particularly—in the offices where paper-pushers toiled, the Director's directive was deeply resented. Corporal Sandy

Seaman, my friend who was a Wharton graduate and had been an insurance actuary before the war, reported to me that his section of examiners of contracts all resented any implication that they were just doing a civilian job at one-tenth what they'd been paid before induction. They held jealously to their ranks in the military. Whatever useful innovations Director Knudson had in mind for Materiel Command, most were strangled at birth. As his directorship masked his actual rank as lieutenant general, any officer above him must have been in the Pentagon, so it's likely the opposition to his civilianization of our duties came from above as well as from below.

Not until reading background material on the P-47 in preparation for this memoir did I learn that Knudson's company, General Motors, with his approval when heading the War Production Board, had persuaded the War Department to fund an experimental fighter, the P-75, to be produced by GM's Fisher subsidiary, which had hitherto manufactured bodies for cars, a firm with no experience in anything aeronautical. The P-75 design was patently inadequate, a wastefully expensive project that had to be aborted. (Bodie's book, from which this information comes [p. 328], is of course partisan to the P-47 and to Republic Aviation, which could have been funded instead to much better advantage.)

Another style of leadership was exemplified by Colonel Donald L. Putt, Deputy Commanding General for the Engineering Division of Materiel Command, who came along later in the war. A West Pointer with overseas experience (he had headed AAF Technical Liaison with Britain), he was at once brusque and approachable. On arrival he made it his business to visit every laboratory and office and speak to each and every person in his command, inquiring what was the work being done and assuring us of his availability had we any suggestions for improvements. More than one of us, struck by this thoroughgoing exploration of our duties, which together constituted his responsibility, had the notion that perhaps a firm like General Motors could learn a thing or two from a really good commanding officer.

In fact, these generals' command comprised two worlds, the

technocratic city on the hillside and the Army post atop the hill. In the Field were, at the bottom, the flight line and hangars, then clusters of buildings each housing either a technical laboratory or a bureaucratic component of the Materiel Command. Here were officers, civilians, and enlisted personnel of all sorts: skilled technicians who operated experiments in wind tunnels, tested the strengths of metals under stress, mounted instruments to measure the efficiency of propellers at differing speeds of rotation, and so on. There were also squads of clerks writing Army specifications for equipment, vetting insurance policies, examining contracts with suppliers. In addition to these professional or specialist personnel, a cadre of enlisted men drove jeeps, delivered messages, were mechanics on the flight line, maintained ground equipment, swept the runways, oversaw traffic and parking, manned the mess halls, and the like. If the aforementioned specialists and technicians were the troops supporting those in combat, these latter were the troops supporting the supporters.

Not all the officers were engineering specialists or, like Captains Ross and Hancock, assigned to bureaucratic supervision of personnel who were. Up on the hilltop were lieutenants whose duty it was to make sure that the men who were housed in the barracks looked and acted like an army. These officers had us out for predawn lineups, had the company clerk post orders with the timetable for inspections, marching drills, calisthenics, and K.P. Every week or ten days everyone lower in rank than technical sergeant served his time peeling potatoes, serving G.I. meals, scrubbing the floor of the mess hall, regardless of the urgency of his unfinished assignments down the hill. And every afternoon, at four, just when thundering summer cloudbursts drenched the men pouring out of the buildings, we'd climb the hill to our spick-and-span barracks to find new assignments from our company clerk. The irrelevance to our actual mission of what G.I.s everywhere called chickenshit was never plainer.

We were housed in wooden barracks two stories tall, with fifty men to a floor. Barracks B was for me an experiment in group living, among men mostly quite different from the college boys I'd known. They were a mixed lot, some few highly qualified and educated technical specialists, plus a lot of men from blue-collar backgrounds doing blue-collar jobs at the Field. We were in this together and had to get along, so most of us did. There were, of course, a few misfits. One was a poor dumb kid who shat in his bed every night and was so indomitably stupid he was the inevitable butt of cruel jokes by those unlucky enough to be bunked near his smelly bed, who had to haul him howling into the showers every morning. It seemed obvious he was a mental defective and had no business in the Army; no doubt his draft board had been hard-pressed to fill their quota.

Among the miscellany of soldiers here I had a few good friends. One was Fred Granberg, a skilled mechanic (he had worked on refrigerators in his other life), a level-headed guy with as much common sense as anyone I'd met. He helped us keep frustrations in perspective. Fred was a pragmatist. One day during our off hours he caught me yet again reading and asked why I always had my nose in a book. I showed him what I was reading, a poem by Rupert Brooke, who at this time was my idea of a war poet. Fred scanned the page.

"This guy is clever, but he doesn't know how to live."

"What makes you say that?"

"Well," Fred said, "he gets excited about things I take for granted."

"For instance?"

"Look at how he goes off the deep end over the leaves turning red in the fall."

"Oh, I think that's beautiful enough to stop and notice, don't you?"

"I don't see the trees raising a sweat over my hair growing longer every month."

"Maybe that's the difference between a man and a tree."

"Ah, go on, you and your education."

Another friend was Sandy Seaman, who spent his days perusing contracts with many, many zeroes after the digits. His views of the modus operandi around us usually coincided with or reinforced my own. Having had several years in an insurance firm, Sandy was both knowledgeable and articulate on the differences between the Army Way and the business way of doing business. Several years older than I, he was married to an admiral's daughter from whom he was in the painful process of being, at long distance, divorced. We had many a beer together.

By one of the inexplicable accidents of Army classification, Leon Goldin, who had studied at the Chicago Art Institute, was actually assigned to the art unit in the Technical Data Branch, where he retouched photographs, drew diagrams, made posters, and performed similar utilitarian functions. This was a grievous underutilization of Leon's talent; in later years he won the Prix de Rome, became a distinguished artist, and headed the painting department in Columbia's School of the Arts. Here at the Field, his duties required him to paint, as it were, only by the numbers.

One fall Sunday afternoon Leon and I set out for some R&R, heading out into the rural landscape. I had brought a pen and notebook, Leon a sketchbook, a little jar of water, and a set of paints and brushes. While I sat on a rock, vainly trying to coax up from nowhere the faint beginnings of a new poem, Leon began to do a watercolor sketch of the woods at the edge of the meadow. In just a few minutes his blank page had vividly evoked the contrasts of dull greens, flaming red and orange of the leaves, the dividing gray and brown trunks amid the abandon of the foliage. Just as I was about to say "Terrific!" Leon suddenly ripped off the painted page, dropped it to the ground, and dipped his brush into one of the color patches to start all over again. I held my tongue and watched—watched him do this over and over again. Half a dozen of what I would have taken home and framed as accomplished landscapes lay at his feet, a few blowing off in the wind. "What are you doing?" I finally asked. "Every good painting," he replied, "is built on the bones of a hundred failures"—a maxim I have remembered and applied to my own work for over fifty years.

While Leon was interpreting the visual pattern and colors of the scene, I was trying to commune with the spirit of the place, in hopes that verbal equivalents to its mood would reveal themselves. The kinship with nature I sought here was something I had deeply missed, I whose boyhood room had stacked boxes of specimen beetles and birds' nests in the bookshelves, a notebook recording sightings of birds over the years, and on the back porch a miniature zoo of captive turtles, garter snakes, a mantis and crickets to feed it, and an ant farm. I eagerly read accounts of natural explorations—Du Chaillu on African jungles, John Muir on American forests—and had read and reread Thoreau. On many a day I explored the shores of Long Island Sound, the reedy flats, the woodlots still standing in Larchmont and New Rochelle. One afternoon, crouched beside Paine Pond in a thicket that served as my blind for observing birds, I'd seen a warbler whose coloration didn't match any in my Peterson guide. I made a quick sketch and, on a trip to New York, called in at the American Museum of Natural History to show my picture to an ornithologist. A curator took me through a long room, not open to the public, with case after case of narrow oak drawers like those used in general stores to hold spools of thread. Opening several of these, he showed me row after row of skinned birds, each with a paper tag tied to one claw identifying the species, place, and date. My sketch matched a sport of the Blackburnian warbler killed at Pound Ridge in 1893.

All told, I was happier off by myself observing the creatures than relating to other kids. Their enthusiasm was for baseball, a game at which I proved inept. In time I came to feel that we humans are parts of a continuum of living creatures, each related to all the others, and I delighted in finding and observing those to be seen in my semisuburban surroundings. But this enthusiasm had been pushed almost out of mind during college in the city and my work at Wright Field. Now all was mechanism, equipment, machines, and theories explaining their operation. And one afternoon in an Ohio meadow didn't suffice to reactivate my imagination. The pages in my notebook were empty.

One Sunday I decided to see what they had on the walls of the Dayton Art Institute. This was an imposing Parthenon-like structure perched on a hilltop at a bend in the Miami River at a distance from downtown Dayton, as though to symbolize its remoteness from the industrial city. The paintings proved unexceptional, though I liked a Hals and a Rembrandt. A pleasant surprise was that they had a Carnegie collection of classical recordings and a listening booth. Better still, this was in the charge of a very attractive girl with green eyes, wavy light brown hair, a fine figure, and a winning smile. She looked more appealing, I thought, than anyone I'd met at the Dayton Service Club. After checking out Vaughan Williams's "Variations on a Theme by Thomas Tallis" and Bach's "Toccata and Fugue in D Minor," I immersed myself for half an hour in a respite from the boredom and frustrations of my quasi-military duties. Returning the albums to the desk, I struck up a conversation. Turned out the keeper of the Carnegie recordings was herself a musician, a pianist. She'd played in a youth concert with the Cincinnati Symphony under Eugene Goosens, and in the fall would study on a scholarship at the Cincinnati Conservatory of Music. We were getting on so well, I asked could I see her outside of the museum, say, next Saturday night? Jeannie seemed as pleased to be found by a fellow who could recognize Beethoven and Brahms as I was to have found her. She lived with her mother (a brother was off in the service) in a small house not far from the center of town. Soon I was spending a lot less time off with Fred, Sandy, or Leon, and none in the Service Club.

★   ★   ★

After having written several hundred abstracts, all chosen, by guess and by God as to their essentiality to our readers, by me, I had the obvious—why did it take so long to think of it?—notion that a questionnaire to the various laboratories could elicit the very topics on which they desired the latest information. Major Ross agreed and had me prepare for his signature a request addressed to the commanding officer of each lab, and then deliver the request myself. This would give me a chance to see the labs at first hand and get a sense of what went on in them.

I was particularly intrigued by Aero Medicine, the latest laboratory to be established on the Field. It was in the next building to Tech Data—we now had a building of our own—but I'd never been inside. A lieutenant showed me around. I was surprised to hear him say he was working in physical anthropology. What, I asked, was the Air Corps's interest in measuring the skulls and bones of dead Indians?

"No, not that. It all began with the P-39."

"The Aerocobra?" I flashed a mental image of the sleek little fighter with a 75-mm cannon in its nose, mounted between the cylinders of its engine—a shape I knew from perusing aircraft recognition posters.

"Yeah. You know, it was designed for high-altitude interception of enemy bombers, could climb five miles in a matter of minutes. Some of the things we're studying here are the physiological effects of such acceleration—how the body adjusts to the tremendous pressure, the loss of oxygen, and so on. Well, did you ever stop to wonder why the P-39 is so famous now as a Russian artillery weapon against tanks?"

"Oh, I thought they bought the planes from us and needed them in the defense of Stalingrad, using whatever they had to knock out the Nazi tanks."

"There's a good reason they had P-39s. When the plane was designed, you know at the Bell plant they made a mockup before starting production. And the president of Bell Aircraft, Larry Bell, climbed into the cockpit, fingered the controls, looked in the gunsight, and said, 'This is great! Let's get started!' So they went right into production, and a couple of months later delivered the first squadron to the Air Force. But there was a problem. The pilots had a lot of trouble getting into the plane.

"Seems Larry Bell was a little guy, about five foot three, weighed maybe 120 pounds. What felt just fine for him—well, the pilots found their ass too big for the cockpit. Since then we've been taking measurements of every air cadet to make sure they can fit into the new model planes they'll fly. Now our physical measurements determine the dimensions of the cockpit, the arrangement of the controls and instruments."

"But how come the Russians could fly the P-39?"

"Oh, they've got a lot of little Laplanders in the Red Air Force. And aren't they lucky we could send them artillery that chases tanks at 300 miles per hour? Makes you feel good that such a costly mistake turned out so well for our gallant ally."

For all I know this story is pure apocrypha, Larry Bell may have been six feet tall and weighed 195 pounds. According to the official history, *The Army Air Force in World War II,* the P-39, designed before the war, was a sluggish little number whose "low ceiling, slow rate of climb and relative lack of maneuverability put its pilots at a decided disadvantage whenever they fought" (VI, 212). So a machine not up to our needs was sold off to the Russians. But the tale of how little-assed Larry Bell O.K.'d a plane we couldn't use made a lot of sense and was firmly fixed in oral tradition.

★   ★   ★

At Wright Field there were small contingents of officers from the air forces of our allies—British, Canadian, Australian, and Russian. The Technical Information Branch of course provided copies of *The Technical Data Digest* to these companions and comrades in the struggle, and we expected that they'd reciprocate by providing our office with technical reports from their countries not available in the journals to which we subscribed. The case of the Purchasing Commission of the Red Air Force was annoying, to say the least. While they were eager for anything of ours they could lay their hands on, they in turn provided us with absolutely nothing. Not a scrap of information about Soviet equipment, Soviet science, Soviet advances in the industrial technologies essential to their war effort.

It was with a great feeling of getting some of our own back when, turning the pages of a newly received British journal, I came on an article describing in detail the LAGG-3 Russian fighter plane. In our December 1943 issue we republished the whole thing, charts, illustrations and all, with this appended note:

> So little information has come from Russia with regard to the design and production of its aircraft that the accompanying article, translated from the Swedish magazine *Flyg,* and based on data from at least three aircraft captured in Finland, will be read with interest. These are among the first details of any Russian airplane to be revealed and were published in the October '43 issue of the British magazine *Aircraft Engineering.*
>
> The article contains some information on the Russian

rocket-assisted bomb. The LAGG-3 is described as the only operational aircraft in service except the British Mosquito which entirely avoids the use of metal.

The LAGG-3, its fuselage of laminated plywood, "is described from Finnish sources as satisfactory in horizontal flight, but with poor acceleration and there is a tendency to go into spin in sharp turns." Nonetheless, it "appears to possess better combat qualities than the earlier MIG-3 fighter."

The allusion to rocket-powered bombs occupies only one paragraph, under "Bomb Racks," where we learn of 25-kg fragmentation bombs, explosive charge in the nose, propelling charge in the body, guided by four stabilizer vanes. "The propelling charge consists of hollow sticks of some apparently slow-burning explosive electrically fired from the cockpit. . . . A case is known where this weapon was used in aerial combat and it is stated that hits have been registered up to 600 m range." At this time we had no comparable weapon; American research on applications of rocketry, undertaken with limited interest and mingy funding, was centered on rocket-assisted takeoffs of overloaded bombers.

It was a great pleasure to publish this scoop on our all too secretive Russian allies.

★   ★   ★

Now, in addition to my writing abstracts, Major Ross (he'd been promoted—and got married the next day) gave me a different assignment. He'd supervised production of a training film on helicopters and thought the script, by Thomas M. Wood, could be published as an article. But a film script, with all its directions to the cameraman and its reliance on visuals to bear the weight of the narrative, is not an article. This one needed a lot of work; I was to rewrite it. For one thing, it wanted some historical background. Of this there was much—the *Bibliography of Rotary Wing Aircraft,* compiled by the Wright Field Library, listed 95 pages of citations from 1863 through April 1944, scores of published accounts of abortive experimental designs for helicopters, autogiros, cycloplanes, gyroplanes. Unfortunately, as this compilation was published after my adaptation of the film script, I couldn't consult it. So off I went to the Aeronautical Library to research Leonardo da Vinci's plans "to make a screw in the air" (the major didn't agree that this phrase would make a good title) and other theoretical and failed practical predecessors of Sikorsky's vertical flying machine. This background would help the reader understand the problems that had to be overcome.

Another special assignment came out of my own mouth. We were receiving a lot of letters requesting referral to abstracts in back issues, and spending a lot of time searching for them. Why not make an index of all the abstracts done each year? No sooner uttered than I was assigned to do the tedious task.

This duty alternated with G.I. rigmaroles on the hilltop. Along with the daily inspections, marching details, and close-order drill and K.P. I've mentioned, the lieutenants assigned to maintain military discipline among us required that we have P.T. All the more needed, you men sit on your ass all day, our D.I. sergeant said. Although I could take a certain physical pleasure in the execution of close-order drill, to the boring, repetitive, obligatory monkey business of calisthenics I had a lifelong antipathy. This must have gone back to childhood, when my father, a great believer in the systematic address to problems, insisted that his underweight, unathletic son be built up by doing push-ups, sit-ups, and the rest, as directed on 78-rpm recordings by the physical culturist Walter Camp. This precursor of today's fitness videos had Camp barking commands, very like our D.I., from our Victrola. But if the machine wasn't constantly rewound, the speed of the turntable gradually, then rapidly, diminished, so that Camp's voice dropped an octave into a stupefied drawl.

In college I'd coped with the Phys. Ed. requirement by volunteering for the freshman wrestling squad, but this proved an unhappy venture. I was too tense to move with a wrestler's instinct, and at my weight, 117, my opponents were inevitably shorter, stockier, quicker. I turned up for practice one day to be confronted by a tiny Asian who in short order had flipped me over, thrown me across the mat, tied me in headlocks and nelsons. Very humiliating, even if, as I learned the next day, he held the 110-lb collegiate championship of Hawaii. Despite this set-back, Coach Waite put me on the frosh team for our first match, against the New York School for the Blind. I thought I'd have the advantage of at least seeing what I was doing. But my opponent, reaching out to touch fingertips as the match began, seemed to have some sixth or seventh sense, knowing always with infallible accuracy not only where I was on the mat but when vulnerable to his much more skillful maneuvers. It was a very strange and unsettling feeling to be soundly defeated by a blind lad, who charged his wrestling with an intensity of purpose as well as a skill I couldn't match.

So I quit the wrestling squad and went out instead for boxing. As there had been a fatality a few years earlier, boxing was no longer an intercollegiate sport but was permitted as an intramural activity. Dick Waite got into his gloves to try me out, and although I'd never boxed, I had a jab of which he approved. Several lessons followed. Once in the service, I always volunteered for boxing as an alternative to P.T.—we'd do roadwork, jogging around the perimeter of the parade ground while the rest of the unit was jumping up and down, spreading legs sideways, touching toes, spreading arms in unison to barked commands.

Only trouble was, there were few other boxers my weight in the Army. We had a match against neighboring Patterson Field, on whose squad the lightest boxer weighed 135 lbs. I was ever being cuffed about the ring. But that was preferable to calisthenics.

In our barracks, at the other end from Leon's and my bunks, was a hard case named—I'll call him Joe DiGiuseppe. I've never met, before or since, anyone who took such pains and pleasure in being obnoxious. DiGiuseppe was forever picking fights and cursing the rest of us. His favorite, much-repeated epithet was "Fuck you, you fucken fuck," an imprecation occasionally alternated with "Go fuck your mother, you fucken fucker." Nobody took this seriously, and within a few days of his arrival in Company B this foul-mouth was known to all as DiGiufuck-enseppe.

He too went out for boxing, not to avoid sit-ups but as an opportunity further to express his aggression. Our coach, a sergeant, arranged practice bouts and served as referee. DiGiuseppe was out of his corner punching the air even before the opening bell, and swarmed all over the poor guy who happened to weigh 165 and so was his designated opponent. This victim could only cover his head with his arms for the three minutes of round one. As the gong struck, he dropped his guard and turned toward his corner. But DiGiuseppe just kept on swinging and landed a huge haymaker right behind the ear of his departing opponent, who crumpled to the floor, knocked out cold. The sergeant grabbed DiGiuseppe from behind, ordered others to strip his gloves off, and barred him from ever setting foot in the ring again.

A few days after that, DiGiuseppe, looking for new targets in the barracks, discovered me. It was a Sunday, and a bunch of us were idling on our bunks, some playing cards, others writing letters. I was writing too, or rather rewriting, and making fair copies of some verses I had, with many corrections and much ear-pulling, eked out to, for, and about my girl. Jeannie had been at the Conservatory for nearly five months now, studying with the renowned piano teacher Léon Conus. But he had suddenly died. Jeannie was heartsick—Mr. Conus had believed in her talent, had made her work hard, and he and his wife were fond of her. To console her I tried to write the sonnet that DiGiuseppe snatched from my bunk, brandished in the aisle, and, mockingly, read aloud in his Brooklyn accent:

      " 'There is no death for those whose life is art'
What the fuck is this?
      'Of youth a hundred years Schubert still sings
      Quietly, as in a world apart,
      Chop-in broods over the haunting strings . . .'
What dya know, Danny-boy's a poet. We got a fucken poet in Barracks B!"

As I tried to snatch the sheet back he held me off and derisively read—

      " 'A hundred souls and hands he taught. 'Tis these
      That give him life whene'er they touch the keys'
Holy shit, this stuff rhymes!"

Swelling with satisfaction, DiGiuseppe ragged me, his derision befouling my idealistic love for my girl. His bullying was center stage now, everyone in the barracks looking on to see how it would play out. Well, a fellow can stand just so much. My mind flashed back to fourth, fifth, sixth grade, when on my way to Chatsworth Avenue School I'd be waylaid by stocky, sneering Bob Otten, a bully whose father had organized a boys' club to rival the Larchmont Boy Scouts; the club, with khaki shirts and shorts, stiff-armed salutes, and military marching, was modelled, it was said, on the youth groups in Germany. For years Bob Otten was the torment of my life—I, a spindly, bookish kid a perfect target. But when we started seventh grade in Mamaroneck Junior High and there he was in my home room, waiting to begin the old humiliation, I suddenly gave him a shove that sent him sprawling across the desk and onto the floor. He never trifled with me again. So I put up my fists to come at my present tormentor, well aware of his advantages in height, weight, and aggressiveness, for the only way to deal with a bully is to have it out with him.

As I drew near his face lit up with anticipation. He dropped my poem, stepped on it, but then suddenly his leer fell off, he let down his own fists, turned, and walked away saying, "Ah, shit, I wouldn't lick a little fucker like you."

Aha, I thought, just shows what a coward this bully is—stand up to him, and he'll fade! Feeling pretty good, I turned to go back to my own bunk and found, standing right behind me with a menacing scowl still on his face, Ernie, six feet tall, famous among us as the light-heavyweight Golden Gloves champion of Minnesota. "I wouldn't let that sonofabitch hurt you," he said. Ernie was indeed a good guy, but still I felt a bit deflated by his protection.

A few weeks later Ernie suffered a couple of cracked ribs. He was on a tall ladder, adjusting something under the wing of a plane, when a corporal driving a jeep down the flight line lost control and crashed into the ladder. Ernie fell some ten feet, his side landing on the fender. So he had his rib cage taped and was advised not to laugh for at least two weeks.

Some time not long after that we had a celebrity visit Wright Field. Billy Conn, who had nearly defeated Joe Louis, was being sent around from base to base to raise the morale of the troops. As a member of our boxing squad I could go to the gym and see the great athlete up close. He travelled with his trainer, cut man, and corner man, all enlisted, all right out of Damon Runyon. Cigars and all, they paid the Army no heed, they were still in the Garden. The way Conn would raise our morale was, he'd take part in an exhibition match against local talent. Our talent was Ernie.

Despite his reluctance to hazard further injury, and aware that Conn outweighed him by probably forty or fifty pounds—the great contender was by no means slimmed down for a championship match; a bulge folded over the top of his trunks—Ernie nevertheless succumbed to demands that, "for the honor of the base," he step into the ring for a three-round exhibition. This was to follow the matches by our squad against boxers from another base. As they had nobody weighing less than 140 lbs, I was spared another thrashing and so sat at ringside for the whole entertainment.

In this hangar cleared of planes, a ring had been set up and folding chairs arranged on all its sides. Ernie, looking very tentative, as though he regretted the whole thing, came down the aisle, climbed in, and acknowledged the encouragement of the men. After a very long pause, preceded by his entourage, Billy Conn entered the ring and smirked to the prolonged applause. Conn had been told all about Ernie's injury and made to promise that he wouldn't hit him in the side—which, newly taped, reflected the lights in a white square. Now our sergeant, mike in hand, climbed in and introduced the fighters in imitation of the palaver of the announcer at the Garden. *Gong!* They touched gloves, backed away, then felt each other out with jabs short of target. Conn stood in the middle of the ring, turning to his right as Ernie danced around him. Conn let fly a jab—Ernie deflected it—then another that caught our man on the chin. But he was backing away so the blow had no force. This went on for what seemed several minutes, then they mixed it up a little. Ernie was doing O.K., he took a couple of punches and landed a couple. He was gaining confidence—here he was in the ring with the guy who was nearly the heavyweight champ of the world—and after three minutes, when the gong struck again, he walked to his corner more assuredly. His buddy, serving as corner man, gave him a swig of water and pumped him up with encouragement. It's hard for a boxer to stay cautious. Hard as he trains, conscious as he is of strategy, of the moves he intends to make or avoid, when in the ring the situation is so fluid he can't consult his brain. He fights on instinct. Training, strategy are of no use unless absorbed into the nerves and muscles; they are manifest unconsciously, for as he ducks and jabs or sees an opening for a hook there's no time to premeditate. *Gong! Round two!* Ernie strides out purposefully, Conn again plants himself in midring. They trade a few jabs—we can see Ernie's confidence grow as he continues exchanging punches with this world-famous boxer who went twelve rounds with the great Joe Louis. For Billy Conn, of course, this is a bore: one of dozens of nights when he stands in the ring with some amateur, not worth getting up a sweat. Conn gets a little careless—there's an opening! Quick-handed Ernie tags him, and has his weight behind the blow. The great Conn is momentarily staggered. The rafters burst with the cheers of the whole cadre watching, but no sooner ejaculated than Conn recovers and smashes his right into that gleaming square of plaster on Ernie's side. End of fight. Ref remonstrates with honored guest, his trainer argues with ref, while Ernie, grimacing, gamely moans he'll go on. But our sergeant leads him away, while we enlisted personnel of Wright Field boost our own morale by booing Billy Conn all the way to the trailer on the flight line that served as his dressing room.

I guess it was too much to expect, that a pro would actually abide by the courtesies of the Marquis of Queensberry and give quarter to an injured opponent rash enough to belt him one. The most salient difference between an amateur and a professional, a champion-caliber pro, is that the pro has a killer instinct and, in the ring, can't tell himself not to let it out. So much for exhibition matches with a celebrity boxer.

A day or so after this fiasco we saw the last of our nemesis DiGiuseppe. The Section Eight he had worked so hard to earn came through, he was discharged and shipped home to Brooklyn. After a month or so he wrote to one of the men he'd bunked next to, saying that the parachute he'd taken home would make a great silk wedding dress for his girl, and would his buddy send him a couple of cartons of free government-issue condoms, since, when married, with us all still in the Army, he planned to fuck all the broads in Brooklyn.

★   ★   ★

Wright Field was an experiment station, and inevitably some experiments were failures. A plywood glider fell apart in midair, spiralled wildly into a pasture, killing the pilot. An experimental engine blew up. And there was another—in fact, two other—crashes involving a major in the photographic unit. He'd made films and taken flying lessons before getting a direct commission and a pair of wings. One day, on an authorized training flight in a plane filled with reconnaissance camera equipment, he had some unaccountable mechanical trouble, crash landed, and caught fire in a field in Indiana. As this was out in the boondocks, no fire department could reach the flames. The major got out all right, but the fuel in his plane exploded, and all that was left was a burnt-out hulk.

About six months later, on another such flight, this same major again had mechanical trouble and crash landed, safely, not very far from the site of his first accident. This was a sparsely populated rural district too, and he had to leave the plane and hike miles to find a farmhouse with a telephone and report his plight. By the time he and the truckload of mechanics sent out from Wright Field got back to the wreck, they found the cameras in it had been stolen. As these were classified military equipment, Air Force Intelligence was put on the case. And it didn't take them long to discover that, wild as that country was, the major owned a few acres out there with a deserted, locked, and boarded-up shack in which, when they broke it open, were found the fancy cameras from both crashes, neatly stored for retrieval and personal use or sale when the war was over.

Another crash had a different cause and different outcome. An experimental fighter was being flight tested, its performance recorded by a camera crew from Tech Data Branch. The takeoff was at noon, and as I was curious to see the new plane fly, I went down to the flight line on my lunch hour, along with the cameramen. The plane taxied to our end of the runway, at the edge of which they had set up their tripods and mounted their cameras. A couple of majors from the lab that developed the plane stood by. It took off, circled above us, then, climbing steeply, headed southwest in the direction of the village of Xenia. Sharply banking, the plane wheeled as though to return, but as we watched, cameras whirring, there was a puff of smoke and the craft began a wild downward spiral—we heard, over the cameras' whirring, whirring, and my heartbeat in my ears, a muffled *boom!*—and a speck was spat out of the smoking plane. The speck fell, fell, fell—"My god," one of the majors cried out, "his chute won't open!" as the cameras whirred and whirred. In a teetering spiral the plane disappeared behind a rise beyond the field. A plume of gray smoke arose, smudging the sky.

One Friday afternoon a lieutenant I didn't know, his chest spangled with ribbons commemorating combat missions, stopped at the door of my office. He'd been seeing to something in the recon photo unit, and now he asked, Would I like to fly with him this weekend to Toronto? We could pick up girls, buy scotch—none available here, our convoys returned from Glasgow with no cases of Johnny Walker, but the Canadians either were able to bring it into their country or had stockpiled warehouses of booze before the war. We, stateside, were reduced to drinking scotch-type likker, a concoction tasting vaguely of kerosene. This invitation was all very tempting, but I didn't want to break a date with Jeannie the following night. So, well knowing this was a once-only opportunity, I put in for a rain check.

Monday morning the whole unit was abuzz—the lieutenant had never reached Toronto, he'd crashed in a blizzard, going the wrong way, in the Pennsylvania mountains. How could a pilot with fifty missions in Italy crash in a snowstorm like that? Those who'd had more contact with bombing missions than I said over there he was flying in formation—only the navigator in the lead plane has to plot the course, the others just follow him, so maybe the lieutenant didn't know how to navigate. Or had instrument failure. Or panicked. In any case, he was killed, and if I'd gone with him, probably I too would have died.

★　★　★

At about this time all enlisted men at Wright Field were interviewed by a panel of officers from another command who were ordered to weed out those not performing essential duties and transfer them to units being trained for combat—that meant the infantry. The Army was preparing for the invasion of Europe. I was duly examined but was passed over. Evidently my duties were considered significant enough for me to remain at Wright Field to do them. But the daily news gave me cause to doubt myself whether my assigned work was indeed significant enough. During the third week of February the Air Force unleashed a series of far-flung bombing raids into Germany itself—pilots of the B-17s and P-47s whose instruction manuals I had helped to prepare were now flying hundreds of missions, attempting to pulverize production of enemy planes. This was the putting to the test Seversky's confident doctrine of strategic bombing, but it was done at great cost. At the time, of course, we were not informed of the rate of losses, but documents reveal them: "American losses were 227 bombers (5.9 percent), British losses 157 bombers (6.7 percent). In addition, U.S. Strategic Air Forces in Europe launched 4,342 fighters, losing 41 (1 percent). More than 5,000 Allied aircrew either died or became prisoners-of-war. More revealing of the intensity of the conflict, however, 1,025 of the 3,823 American bombers credited with sorties against the enemy suffered damage" (McFarland and Newton, *To Command the Sky,* 190).

Even without these appalling numbers as yet in the public domain, it was obvious that mass bombings could not be undertaken without risk. The thought of squadrons of Messerschmitts swooping out of the sun to attack our fighter escorts, and our B-17s having to fly through skies littered with flak, some of our planes hit by enemy fire and exploding in midair or pluming ablaze to the ground, made war in the air as hazardous as the trench warfare of World War I. Pilots, bombardiers, flight engineers, gunners, all were vulnerable, all were at risk in moving targets from which there was no escape until the lucky survivors returned from hostile skies. While this was happening over Germany, I was still editing a magazine in Dayton, Ohio.

★   ★   ★

The success of the helicopter article led Major Ross to propose that in each issue, along with the abstracts, we publish a feature full-length article "on a current aeronautical development of general interest" by a staff member of one of the laboratories. Major Ross had me draft a letter for Colonel Hayward's signature to the commanding officers of each lab, requesting their cooperation. It wasn't at all a foregone conclusion that those colonels would see the advantage in taking one of their best men off actual research to write an article for Major Ross's magazine. In the meantime, while awaiting their responses, I had come upon something especially interesting.

We received all the available British aeronautical literature. I particularly liked reading those journals, so elegantly printed; *The Aeroplane* made a vivid contrast to the tabloid layout and demotic prose style of the American *Aero Digest*. The English magazine expressed technical truths with concision and editorialized with irony, a sort of writing I would later find, in other contexts, in *The New Statesman* and *Spectator*. Reading the *Journal of the Royal Aeronautical Society* had its surprises; in the personal notes, on members, along with notices of the promotions in the armed forces or civilian job changes of British aerodynamicists, there were similar entries for German members of the Royal Society, and regrets at reports of the illness or deaths of Nazi scientists now designing planes the better to bomb Britain. The pursuit of scientific knowledge, it seemed, was above mere politics or faction; all members of the R.A.S. were linked in a brotherhood not to be diminished by the applications others might make of their discoveries. I found nothing comparable to this point of view in American scientific literature.

The most recent *Journal of the Royal Aeronautical Society*

(December 1943) had a curious item: translation from the German of a paper in *Flugsport u. Wehr Technik* for 1941 by one J. Stemmer. This was a historical survey of rocketry and an explanation, with scores of equations, of its principles and those of jet engines. Could there be any connection to another German article, from *Flugsport,* 1939, translated in *Aircraft Engineering* (February 1942) on "Thermal-Air Jet-Propulsion"? And I came on articles in *Aero Digest* and *Air Force* magazines for January–March 1944 describing a plane that flew without a propeller and had a most unconventional engine. It produced combustion so strong it propelled the aircraft.

I showed these to Major Ross—here were two kinds of jet propulsion, one in which oxygen was chemically fused to the fuel; in the other, oxygen from the atmosphere was ignited in a spray of aviation gas. While awaiting articles from the labs, I suggested, I might be able to put these reports together.

But first Major Ross required me to consult with the head of our Power Plant Laboratory, to get his views. The colonel patiently heard me out, then leaned back and smiled. "This is all nonsense. What kind of a dreamer would think up a plane with no propeller, or aim a rocket so it could land exactly a hundred miles away? But if Major Ross wants you to write up this Jules Verne stuff, go ahead—don't let me stop you."

This conversation was puzzling indeed. Was this colonel blindly committed to the reciprocating engine? And was his skepticism real or dissembled? As I learned after the war, reading *Jet: The Story of a Pioneer* (1953), by Sir Frank Whittle (the inventor of the British jet that was the subject of a couple of the sources for my article), as early as September 1941, before Pearl Harbor, there was Anglo-American cooperation on jet engine research—the W.1.X engine (now in the Smithsonian Institution) was flown to the States and was used as a basis by General Electric engineers for a modified model. The Bell Aircraft Corporation in Buffalo already had under construction three prototypes of the P-59 aircraft, to be jet-propelled. Sir Frank wrote (this passage is undated but precedes one for July 7, 1942), "During a visit to the U.S. Army Air Force Experimental Base at Wright Field near Dayton, Ohio, I had many talks with senior technical officers. From the Commanding Officer, Brigadier General Vannaman, downwards, their enthusiasm for the jet engine was impressive, and there already existed plans for test equipment on a scale far greater than anything we contemplated in Britain. Indeed, a plant for testing jet engines under high-altitude conditions was already under construction" (222).

Although this work was top-secret, is it likely that the commanding officer of the Power Plant Laboratory at Wright Field would have been unaware of what was going on in his own field? And by late 1943 mention of jet propulsion could not have been top secret, or even secret at all, for there had been reports in the press of German developments. Swedish sources revealed a "pilotless armada" being built preparatory to bombing London (*New York Times,* August 26, 1943, p. 9), reports repeated on December 5 (p. 5) and again on December 14 (p. 1) from Swiss sources. On our side, Whittle wrote: "Shortly before the end of 1943 . . . under pressure from the U.S. Government, it had been decided that some official disclosure of Allied work on jet engines should be made" (259), and in the New Year's Honours List, 1944, R.A.F. Flight Commander Whittle, as he then was, received the C.B.E. and instant celebrity. So Allied development work on jet propulsion, though its details were classified, could hardly have been secret, or unknown to high-ranking officers engaged in research at Wright Field.

As for the other variety of jet propulsion, rocketry, already in the 1930s "one government (Hitler's Germany) recognized the potential military significance of rockets." I quote from Andrew G. Haley's historical survey *Rocketry and Space Exploration* (Princeton, 1958): "In 1933, the German Army established the world's first coordinated guided missile research center at Peenemunde. . . . Here, in the next decade, would be gathered the cream of Germany's technical brainpower to work on every phase of research and experimentation that had any bearing on guided missiles, not the least important of which was rocket propulsion" (44, 47).

Yet "despite the double-pronged Government effort in Germany and claims of ambitious projects in Russia, the United States Government still exhibited little official interest in rocketry" (57–58). Apparently this was equally true of Britain, for Haley has nothing to say of developments there. It appears that Stemmer, author of the article I found translated in the *Journal of the Royal Aeronautical Society,* was but a minor figure in German rocket research. He appears in Haley's book only in two group photographs, along with a score of other scientists.

I had to wonder, perhaps the chief of Power Plant was putting me on. He must have known that although reports of such developments were by then appearing, nearly all Air Force personnel were uninformed, and the article I proposed, based on unclassified material, would help to familiarize its readers with inevitable developments. And yet it was the Army Air Corps command who, since the mid-1930s, had stubbornly backed the in-line, liquid-cooled engine (which made the P-51 vulnerable to hits in its cooling system) and denied funding for development of the radial Pratt and Whitney air-cooled engine and supercharger that gave the P-47B its power. The Germans already had developed such refinements for the Focke-Wulf 190 (Bodie, 147). So the colonel commanding Power Plant in 1944 may have still had the mindset of five to ten years earlier.

In any case, I went to work, combining elements abstracted from half a dozen sources into a unified exposition, "Pure and Thermal Jet Propulsion," with diagrams illustrating how both jet engines and rockets operate. I offered discussion of their advantages over reciprocating engines, their respective drawbacks, the gain in efficiency from eliminating propellers and in aircraft design for jet power, as well as noting attendant problems—difficulties at supersonic speeds, metallurgical requirements for such high temperatures. This appeared in the April 1944 issue of *The Technical Data Digest,* "Prepared by Sergeant Daniel G. Hoffman, Technical Information Branch, Technical Data Laboratory, Engineering Division." My first article in a national magazine.

Two months later, on June 13, the first V-1 "robot" bombs struck London, airborne missiles carried by pilotless jets, terrifying the populace, landing at random on sites of civilian life. This fearful weapon was shortly followed by the V-2, a flying bomb propelled by rockets. Too small to be a target for antiaircraft fire, and launched from mobile ramps that constant R.A.F. and

American Air Force bombing raids on the French coast could not eliminate, the V-1 could be brought down by pilots in their Spitfires or Hurricanes flying parallel at 300 mph, then closing in and, in a sudden roll, lifting the fighter's wing under that of the buzzbomb, flipping it into a dive. Even then it might land on and blow up a town or a farmhouse.

The Nazis' reliance on these unmanned missiles reflected the damage Allied bombing had done to their aircraft production and the toll AAF and R.A.F. fighters had taken of their pilots. The British must have had intelligence that the V-2 (and possibly V-1) was long under development, for Stemmer's article described its prototype. But reprinting his detailed piece in the *Journal of the Royal Aeronautical Society* came too late for the R.A.F to mount a counterweapon. While Stemmer and a whole cadre of rocket and jet propulsion scientists were being taken seriously in the 1930s by administrators of both the Luftwaffe and the German aviation industry, here in our country the pioneering rocket inventor R. H. Goddard was dismissed as a science-fiction hobbyist who played with fireworks.

As for aircraft powered by jet engines, the Germans and the British had these in action in 1944. The Messerschmitt 262 was powered by a turbojet engine, the Me.163 by rockets, and "began to be a serious menace especially to the daylight bombing operation of the U.S. Army Air Force . . . on one occasion when the Americans lost 32 out of a formation of 36 Flying Fortresses" (Whittle, 278–79). The British jet, the Meteor, was "temporarily withdrawn from combat . . . and used in tactical trials with British based American bomber and fighter formations . . . to evolve defensive tactics against the Me.262." These trials proved the existing aircraft helplessly vulnerable to attack by jet-powered fighters. "The German crews and some of their leaders had been anticipating a miracle. On May 28 [1944] . . . the Führer directed that, for the time being, the Me.262 was to be used only as a high-speed bomber. . . . Hitler's decree highlighted once again his irrational interference in military technology as well as strategy and tactics" (McFarland and Newton, 236). So Hitler's insane egotism protected the Allied aircraft from the Nazi jet fighter.

Trials in the U.S. with our experimental jet models, the Bell P-59 and Lockheed P-80, corroborated the tests in England. But our fighters with jet engines didn't come off their production lines until the war was over. The AAF flew prop-driven aircraft clear to the end, suffering losses avoidable had our jet fighters been combat-ready in 1944 and 1945.

★   ★   ★

One day Major Ross called me in to his office. "How'd you like to go for a flight, take a flying lesson, Dan?" He had just received his civilian pilot's license. Since flying was not part of his military assignment, he'd taken lessons at his own expense from a civilian instructor, and now he'd take me up in the plane. And let me have a go at flying it. I, who had written instructions for the pilots of P-47s, had never actually done this myself, but surely flying a little trainer would be a piece of cake. I'd been a passenger several times, hitching rides home on furloughs in DC-7s, and once with a British pilot whose plane ferried embassy personnel between Washington, New York, and Wright Field. (We flew—with me in the copilot's seat, wearing the headphones—to Floyd Bennett Field; when, many years later, I read my poems at Nassau County Community College, I recognized the president's house as the former manse of the Commanding General, and faculty houses had been Officers' Row. We approached New York a couple of days after a B-25, in deep fog in those pre-radar days, had crashed into the Empire State Building; those earphones crackled with instructions from the tower at Floyd Bennett, keeping a dozen craft circling Long Island for over half an hour to be sure not to hit any tall buildings.) But this flight with Major Ross would be my first in a small plane.

The airport was a cleared meadow, the runway marked out with whitewash, the hangar a barn, a windsock flying from a stick in the ground. The plane was a little two-seater biplane with dual controls. We climbed in, buckled up, and Major Ross let the engine warm up, it and the propeller roaring loudly. Then he taxied down the meadow and we took off. The fragility of the plane, the sizzle of the air going over the windshield, the buzz of the engine, the propeller's roaring swish, all crowded my impressions. "O.K., Dan, you take over," and I grabbed the stick, feeling its resistance. My least movement resulted in a jerky divagation, tipping us off level or off course, errors requiring immediate correction. But moving the stick the other way made the plane tip crazily in reverse to where it had gone before, and the nose suddenly was pointing down. Some twenty years after the event I wrote it up this way, fantasticating a few details for effect:

First Flight

I watches me climb
in the cockpit, him fixing
the belt and moving
my hand I see

the prop rev and the plane
cough forward
both wings biting
sudden wind

I on ground invisible
sees me taxi obvious
behind him Wild Pilot
what I doing there & here

particularly when
up high he says
Dan,
he says, Dan boy,

take over I don't feel
too good after all
that Scotch-type rot
last night I'm flying

me at the joystick o
boy how come
those chickens getting bigger chasing
their shadows under stoops

I see it clearly
clearly
STICK BACK!
and we climb

higher than the sun
sinking in a stew of clouds
Well Major anything
for a laugh me say

I say let's bring her down

Of course the major was cold sober, nor did I come close to crashing—inventions to intensify presentation of the experience, make it psychologically arresting. In that cockpit I now knew that intellectual knowledge of what to do is one thing, physical ability to do it quite another. And although one can't learn to fly in only one lesson, that's long enough to feel the doubleness of consciousness, both in and out of the predicament, when confronted by perceived danger. Landing at last, I got out of the trainer a bit less cocky than when I'd climbed in.

★ ★ ★

Major Ross summoned me again. "Dan," he said, "Word has trickled down to us from the higher echelons. They've decided the *Digest* should be headed by an officer." And who would that be, of course ran through my head, someone already here, or a stranger we'd have to break in and get used to?

"So, I've been thinking, the best officer to head the *Digest* would be you. Only thing is, you're not an officer—yet. Now you go and apply to O.C.S."

Several weeks later I was on detail on the hill, carrying coal through the snow into the barracks for the stove, when summoned to my O.C.S. examining board. Two majors, three captains, and two lieutenants. I saluted and stood at attention.

They began with some questions on general orders, basic training stuff. I knew that cold, but it was fishing in a vacuum; I couldn't summon up a thing. "I don't know that, sir. No excuse."

Captain A.: Are you nervous before this board of review?

I don't think so, sir. If I am, it's an involuntary reaction. (Captain smiled.)

They asked about the work I do, about the Jordanoff manuals, how they differ from other manuals.

Captain B.: What's the matter with manuals as they are written now?

I explained their inadequacies.

Major B.: Jordanoff jazzes up his books so the men will read them, doesn't he?

The effort, sir, is to make the material interesting.

Captain A.: What do you think of John Dewey?

I'm not familiar enough with his work to give an opinion, sir.

Capt. A.: Who is? Can you name some of his writings?

Democracy in Education. Human Nature and Conduct. A Common Faith.

Capt. A.: Have you read any of them?

I've read A Common Faith, and excerpts from the others.

Major A.: This pilot's manual, did any fliers check it, or did you do it alone?

That, sir, was a revision of one previously prepared by the Republic Corporation and Air Service Command for the P-47B. With the modifications in the model C, it was felt advisable to revise the instructions and put them in the form developed by Jordanoff. The material was taken from observation and interviews, from the old manual, and from consultations with engineers at Republic. It was carefully read over by Republic's test pilots. The manuscript was approved here at Materiel Command before it was printed.

Major A.: Do you find your technical background sufficient to understand the material you read?

Although my formal engineering education isn't extensive,

I've picked up a fairly good background from my work. I seldom have trouble understanding the principles of the material I've covered. While, for instance, I don't have a knowledge of the electrical theory behind the operation of an autopilot, I understand the way it works well enough to explain it to someone else.

Major B.: Do you think you can write better manuals than are now being produced?

Yes, sir!

Captain B.: Why do you want to be an officer instead of a noncommissioned officer?

I hope to make my training available in the most effective way to the Air Corps, and at present the responsibilities I can undertake are considerably limited by my rank.

Captain A.: If you were assigned to a desolate outpost, which three books would you bring with you?

Aristotle's Complete Works, Chaucer's Canterbury Tales, and Gargantua and Pantagruel by Rabelais.

Captain B.: Why didn't you apply for pilot training?

Sir, I thought seriously about that. When I was on inactive enlisted reserve, I was urged by officers from here at Wright Field to see Lt. Col. Hodge, the Public Relations Officer of the Eastern Procurement District, and discuss my work at Jordanoff with him. I asked whether in his opinion I should enlist in combat training, either ground or air, or whether that experience was valuable enough to the Army for me to hope to be assigned to some related line of duty. On his advice and with his assistance, I was sent here to Materiel Command.

Captain A.: As a student of philosophy, what, in your opinion, is the gravest problem confronting a private in the Army?

For some men there is no problem at all. Some can find themselves in a regulated routine existence and, not being reflective or analytical, they'll have no difficulty in making a satisfactory adjustment. Others find it hard to have their thinking done for them and their time occupied with unimportant and unpleasant tasks. For them it's a problem of self-discipline.

They asked would I do a good job as a mess or supply officer. I said I'd do the best I could but would hope my training would fit me for a more appropriate assignment. Could I handle people older than myself? Everyone on my staff is older than I, and I've never had any trouble. Thank you, sergeant. Dismissed.

Talking over the review board experience with other prospective O/Cs, I heard what they were asked: Who are the full generals in the U.S. Army? How many men in a squadron? What's base pay for a second lieutenant? If you were post commander, how would you improve conditions on this field? Describe a B-25. Who's your commanding officer?

My board instead put me through a cross between a job interview and an oral course exam at college. And who was Captain A., who asked me about John Dewey, and which books I'd take to a desert? If commissioned, I'd like to look him up and have a few beers, but I never learned the names of my examiners. Of the 115 men examined, ten made scores of 80 or above; two others and I got 83, and soon received orders to report to O.C.S. in San Antonio. I had mixed feelings. I looked forward to becoming officer in charge of the *Digest* but was reluctant to leave Jeannie for two long months. When the time came, promises to one another of frequent letters did little to allay regret in a lingering farewell.

★ ★ ★

Officer Candidate School was not in San Antonio, it was in a sun-baked stretch of desert miles outside the city. The barracks were ovens, the unbearable heat stoically borne. Colonies of two-inch roaches found homes in our sweaty boots and puttees. Tarantulas prowled underneath the barracks. A heavy schedule of classes was to produce instant expertise—six hours of military law and, if required, we could each hold a court-martial. Classes in everything from small-arms fire to administration of a squadron; we were being prepared for all the administrative roles a second lieutenant might have to fill. This cram education was sandwiched between a lot of chickenshit imitated from West Point: candidates in our class obliged to salute upperclassmen who had been there only a couple of weeks longer than we; required to take meals in angular positions, respond to summonses to fall in at all hours of the night, and such like nonsense. Also, lots of close-order drill. The aims of this curriculum were divided against each other, since we were being trained simultaneously for unthinking obedience and for leadership with initiative. It's a challenge, trying to change men's character in only a few weeks.

As we in turn became upperclassmen, rank had its privileges: we were given moments of time off. On Sundays we'd be bussed in to San Antonio, deposited at the marquee of a posh hotel beside the piddling stream that divides the city, and go inside to a tea dance with the fairest daughters of the Lone Star State. Their mothers ordinarily wouldn't let these young ladies within ten yards of a Yankee, but since we, as officer candidates, were certified as gentlemen, the girls were permitted to dance with us on these occasions for which no sequels were possible.

Toward the end of our candidacies we were sent on maneuvers. Divided into squadrons, we set up camp in the desert, pitched tents, decontaminated oil drums of water with chlorine tablets, slept in the sagebrush to the music of coyotes, and marched through the arroyos under orders on missions whose purpose was undisclosed, bearing full kit and gear in the heat. It was here that the words of Izzy Diamond came back to haunt me, for one of the lieutenants in charge had read my record and appointed me O/C Communications Officer. I was to generate a daily news sheet to keep up morale—that meant making laborious humor of our discomforts and boosting the spirit of the maneuvers, on a portable typewriter and a hand-cranked mimeograph machine. This was dog-work writing, yet one page I composed out there in the sagebrush brought more instant recognition and enthusiastic acclaim than anything I've written since. I had shared the exhausting routine and noticed that outgoing mail was getting sparser and fewer. So was the number of incoming letters. Although feigning combat conditions, we had regular mail calls, pickups and deliveries by jeep bringing bags of letters that had arrived at the barracks. It occurred to me that each of the men had a wife or girlfriend to whom he was just too bushed to write, and from whom he was perhaps therefore not getting mail.

So I composed an all-purpose love letter, in which G.I. jokes about our plight among the tarantulas and rattlers and assurances that we were being transformed into first-rate officers alternated with assertions of undying devotion. All the sender had to do was to fill in the blank after "Dearest . . ." and sign his own name on the line that followed "With all my love." I was assured by just about every man in that desert that this document met a deeply felt need. I sent a copy to Jeannie to remind her it had been quite a while since I'd heard from her, and stowed another in my gear as a souvenir. But as is the case with so much of life's ephemera, the letter disappeared long ago, so I've had to describe it from memory.

At last, graduation. I had made the acquaintance, halfway through the course, of the post librarian, whose aid I'd solicited to help me find a novel of Hemingway's not in place on the shelves. He seemed pleased indeed that an O/C would have such reading in mind, and started a conversation. Soon it became apparent that the librarian, M/Sgt. Irwin Stock, was himself a writer of fiction, indeed had published short stories. At graduation, his wife Phyllis pinned my new gold bars on my collar and invited me to their apartment for a congratulatory bottle of wine and a home-cooked dinner. After the war I corresponded for a time with Irwin, came on his fiction in some of the better quarterlies, and read reviews praising his pioneering study of the Victorian novelist Mark Rutherford. But Irwin was teaching in Florida, a state I didn't revisit for fifty years, and as is often the way with friends long separated, we lost touch.

A few days after graduation I received orders to report to Dayton, Ohio.

III

THIS time I got off the bus at Wright Field not as a green private ignorant of what his duties would be, but as the officer to be in charge of "the official journal of the AAF Research & Development Program." First I had to report again to the C.O. of the entire Technical Data Laboratory, Colonel J. M. Hayward. Although as an enlisted man I'd had virtually no contact with him, he welcomed me warmly and said, "Lieutenant, I have in my closet a uniform I used to wear when I was as trim as you— as you can see, I haven't been able to get into it in a long time. I'd like you to have it." This was a thoughtful and generous gesture, for officers are responsible for their own kit, and a new lieutenant, ordering several changes of shirts and slacks and a jacket and a dress uniform as well, would run up quite a bill at the haberdasher's before receiving his first officer's paycheck.

Next I called on Lt. Col. B. A. Davis, Hayward's deputy, Assistant Chief for Informational Branches, who was directly above Major Ross. Next I was welcomed back by the major and by my co-workers, now my staff. Then I went downstairs to the art unit to greet Leon. "About two weeks after you left," he said, "I ran into Jean one evening in Dayton. She told me she'd taken a night job to keep her mind off missing you so much." That was reassuring, for the frequency of her letters had dwindled in the past month. My reporting for duty completed, I hastened to call her up, savoring how we'd enjoy my taking her for the first time to the Officers' Club at Patterson Field (there was none at Wright). At last I poured into the phone my hoarded-up relief at being close to her again. She said she'd missed me too, but I could tell she was holding something back. She couldn't see me until the following evening.

Disappointed and baffled, I occupied that day and the next as I had to, then hurried in to Dayton for the long-awaited reunion. Jeannie looked just as I'd remembered her, but pale and tense. Before I could say anything, she said, "We won't be able to see each other anymore." What was she saying? She was telling me she was engaged. Engaged? How was that possible? Engaged to a captain from Patterson Field. And she handed me a parcel: all my letters and the photo she had implored me to give her just before I left for O.C.S. She was impatient, wanted this interview to be over and done with. There was no more to say. Indeed there was no more; a few months later I read about her wedding in the *Dayton Daily News*.

Stunned, I returned to the Bachelor Officer Quarters in a daze and tried to puzzle out what had happened, to her, and to me. In the B.O.Q. such contemplation was impossible. Every night silence was shredded by boisterous laughter, expostulations at poker games, and other disturbances in the adjoining cubicles. Officers were permitted to live off base, but for that I would need transportation. I was relieved to notice an ad in the Dayton paper—a car for sale at a nearby garage. For a hundred dollars I became the owner of a 1928 Model A. This durable vehicle was mechanically simple, the only car I've ever owned on which I could change the engine gasket myself.

I now looked around for digs. A dozen miles away was the village of Yellow Springs. Here were brick schoolhouses and churches in Greek Revival architecture—Ohio had been the Western Reserve, settled from Connecticut—and a cluster of nineteenth-century frame houses around the buildings of Antioch College. I learned that Professor Geiger had a room available, so I moved in and stayed for a month, until his aged mother came to live with them. Then I found a room at 509 Xenia Avenue, in the home of an elderly widow, Mrs. Dean. Through George Geiger, who taught philosophy, I met several other faculty members, mostly his fellows on the board of the *Antioch Review.* The editor of this quarterly was the college librarian, Paul Bixler. With his contributors scattered across the globe in the services, Paul was short of material for future issues. Learning that I had studied at Columbia, he asked if I had anything the magazine could consider.

As a matter of fact, I did. In the spring of sophomore year, before my Jordanoff work, I'd taken a course in advanced composition with Frederick Dupee. We met three times a week, and the first assignments were to write a paragraph for each meeting. The following week, a page. Thus we worked our way up toward a two-month-long major project, an essay of some length. This was my opportunity to make academic capital of an enthusiasm I'd had for several years. In high school I'd taken up the clarinet and joined a little band that tried to play Dixieland as well as standard pop arrangements. We weren't much good, never got gigs, but I persisted although not nimble enough to perform to anyone's satisfaction. Once in college I'd had to give it up, since I had no time to practice. But I'd become an aficionado of early jazz, New Orleans through Chicago Style, and read and reread the books then available: Robert Goffin's, and Hugues Panassié, whose *Le Jazz Hot* had recently been translated. I'd gone as far as Cos Cob to attend jam sessions, and while at Columbia hung out at downtown jazz clubs, the Village Vanguard and Nick's. I'd write the history of jazz for Mr. Dupee.

Fred Dupee was intrigued by my topic, for, he told me, he'd gone to high school in Chicago with Muggsy Spanier, Frank Teschmaker, and the others who were doing something exciting, but what it was he hadn't known. I drew on the books and on my small but carefully chosen record collection (I'd haunted record shops, gone without lunches in high school to buy 78s discarded from jukeboxes), and field recordings by Alan Lomax and Harold Courlander in the music library. At Nick's in the Village, in a break between sets, I bought a drink for the New Orleans clarinettist Edmund Hall and told him of my project. He invited me to his apartment in the Bronx to hear his records going back to King Oliver.

My theme was how jazz evolved from the fusion of different musics. Negroes before the turn of the century played old Civil War band instruments, adapting to them the vocal style of their blues and hollers. Louis Armstrong's trumpet solos were of a piece with his scat singing. In New Orleans this music was enriched by musicians trained to play in the orchestras of opera companies, with embouchures from classical music influencing jazz performance—evident, for instance, in the contrast between the clarinet styles of blues-influenced Johnny Hodges and the much smoother playing of Omer Simeon. When this music went upstream, Fred Dupee's classmates heard Louis Armstrong in Chicago, and they, who had taken classical lessons, now played jazz, further extending its range of styles. Not only was the music played by both blacks and whites, but its structure embodied the rewarding tension between individual solos and ensemble playing. In the latter, group improvisation seemed to threaten anarchy and dissolution, yet it was held together not only by its rhythm but by the shared traditions in which each instrumentalist participated. The music embraced exuberant joyousness and also the sufferings and griefs of the blues. Jazz of this sort was a folk-based chamber music, a community of artistic expression. And anyone present during a jam session who understood the dynamics of the music could feel himself a part of that community.

This went on for nearly a hundred pages. I sent home for the text, spent several weekends revising and condensing it to some twenty-five pages, then gave it to Bixler. He passed it around to his board, and after a couple of weeks told me they'd agreed to accept it. In the spring of 1945, the *Antioch Review* contained my essay, "The Folk Art of Jazz." In later years I wrote several further, more sophisticated studies along this line.

★ ★ ★

In our August 1944 issue *The Technical Data Digest* gained a new look. Linotyped copy replaced varityping, two columns per page gave way to three, and thereafter the cover of each issue presented a photograph of a new technical development of the Engineering Division (though this first issue in the new format featured a picture of our then chief of the Engineering Division, Brigadier General F. O. Carroll).

This new format gave a professional appearance to our journal. The back cover listed abbreviations of the publications in the Technical Data Library from which abstracts in each issue were prepared. The inside front cover described the photo on the front; the contents page was followed by a column the major or I prepared each month, "What's in the Air for [the month]," calling attention to particularly significant topics abstracted and to the feature article. This column occupied only a quarter of the space on the page, leaving plenty of room for what were supposed to be eyecatching illustrations. These, however, made up by someone in the title unit of the Training Film Branch, were cobbled together from stencilled lettering and such stock images as displaying the copy on the pages of an open book or, as in the August issue, beneath the silhouette of an airplane. I determined to give Leon an assignment more stimulating, I hoped, than the routine stuff he was doing downstairs, stencilling titles for films and manuals. In the first page he designed, "What's in the Air for November" presented its printed message in the lower left-hand quarter of the page. Above it hovered a dual-rotored helicopter flying in an irregular cloud from which rays descended to the right, concentrating in another such cloud in which a large, primitive dual-rotored craft of ancient design hovered near the ground. Concentric lines on the ground, spreading out toward the bottom of the page, echoed those in the sky.

The following month, December 1944, Major Ross's column observed the fourteenth anniversary of *The Technical Data Digest* and went on to comment on the progress of aviation since the Wright brothers' first twelve-second flight, forty-one years before. Midway up the right side of the page, Leon provided a semiabstract rendering, against a dark background, of the tower at Kitty Hawk, its beacon sending a beam diagonally up to the left and illuminating a large image of a B-17, while at the base of the tower were large busts of Wilbur and Orville. Radiating lines again emanated from beneath one of the brothers toward the bottom of the page, left, center, and right; above one of these rays hung the tiny white silhouette of the first airborne craft.

These illustrations, their treatment of perspective subliminally suggesting the infinite expansion of aeronautical knowledge, were faintly evocative of Yves Tanguy's surrealism and greatly enhanced the appearance of our journal. Major Ross and I looked forward to many months' issues similarly emblazoned by that talented corporal downstairs.

During these months, October–December, American armies attacking Aachen and the Hürtgen Forest in what was later known as the Battle of the Bulge were encountering fierce enemy resistance, wretched wet weather, and conditions in the nearly impenetrable forest terrain that made our tanks and fighter-bombers useless. Casualties were horrendous—the Keystone Division lost 6,184 men, the 112th Infantry, 2,093 (Russell Weigley, *Eisenhower's Lieutenants* [Bloomington, 1981], 320–69). Reports of the appalling battle conditions and heavy losses reached us in the newspapers and in *Life* magazine. Leon and I pored over the terrible news, well aware that among the casualties there were bound to be friends and former classmates. What could we do but try to fulfill our own assigned duties as well as possible, though the eventual effect on the war of the engineering literature and instructional materials we wrote and illustrated would be indirect and delayed. The Battle of the Bulge, and other battles overseas, would go on without us. This knowledge was unsettling.

Just about then a team of officers seeking new recruits to replace the casualties we were reading about made another pass through Wright Field. Leon shipped out for infantry training the following month.

★   ★   ★

A brief article in the local paper caught my eye: Gerald L. K. Smith would speak that weekend in nearby Cedarville. I had never heard this rabble-rouser, and determined to go, out of uniform, and bring along a pen and notebook so I could take down what he said in speedwriting, a form of shorthand I had last used to take notes in Irwin Edman's lectures on aesthetics. (I typed up my record of the speech and gave the typescript to Paul Bixler for the college library. Half a century later it couldn't be found, but Ms. Nina D. Myatt of the library staff kindly sent me a xerox of an issue of the student newspaper reporting a Smith rally at a nearby fairground a week earlier, virtually the same speech as what I recalled.)

There were maybe a hundred people, mostly men, most of them farmers, some blue-collar workers in overalls, and maybe a dozen or a score of soldiers in uniform in the grandstand in the woods—probably the athletic field of tiny Cedarville College; this was at night and I couldn't make out much of the surroundings. The speech was sponsored by several like-minded organizations: Christian War Veterans (of WWI), Youth for Christ, the Farmers' Guild, and Constitutional Mothers. These, I believe, were all front cadres for the America First movement, the isolationists who had opposed our entry into the war.

All, especially the civilians, looked hard-used by life, men whose unending toil had not been well rewarded. Smith was tall, large, beak-nosed, tossing his mane of hair, gesticulating as he spoke in the mounting periods of a revivalist preacher. His was a primitive style, but it captivated this crowd. His message was that President Rosenfeld had betrayed them by luring this country into war, a war being waged for the profit of Jews on Wall Street. These Jews were in a conspiracy with Europe to suck out the value of their hard-earned dollars. George Washington, he said, had paid for the American Revolution with money borrowed from Haim Solomon, "and we'll be paying the interest on that loan for the next two hundred years." Somehow, the Revolutionary War loan was a conspiracy of European Jewish Communists to cheat hard-working, God-fearing Americans of their birthright.

This rant hit the right buttons in that grievance-ridden crowd of losers, people to whom wartime prosperity had delivered nothing. How many of them had known any Jews? There surely were few if any Jews in Cedarville or the other little villages in southern Ohio, and, I doubted, many in Dayton or Springfield. But persons seeking others to blame for their own misfortune or incompetence don't need actual Jews, who in any case are all on Wall Street conspiring to keep them in poverty forever.

Jews were not Smith's only target—"The two biggest scandals in American history are about to break: one, Pearl Harbor; two, Tylor Kent, a young clerk in England working for the American embassy. He decoded messages between Churchill and Roosevelt" revealing that those two planned the war in 1938 and 1939. At Pearl Harbor, Smith asked, "Why were 8,000 boys killed? [Admiral] Kimmel and [General] Short were not to blame." The disaster was part of Roosevelt's plan to bring America into the war.

"Let's go with men like Thomas Jefferson, Hamilton Fish, Father Coughlin, Abraham Lincoln, Gerald L. K. Smith, and Jesus Christ." At the end of this diatribe Smith called out, "Don't leave, people—anyone who leaves now is either sick or a Communist! You people there at the entrance—Have you all got envelopes? . . . Everybody who gives $10 gets to keep the pencils."

Smith worked them up into an ugly mood, and had there been an identifiable Jew or two in the stands they'd doubtless have gone after them with clubs and rope. A week earlier, at a similar rally in Celina, Smith had slapped, and several of his cadre had shoved, a couple of Antioch students who were distributing leaflets for the liberal Farmers' Union just outside the fairgrounds after the rally; the students were self-disciplined, kept cool, and didn't provoke further violence. Now the crowd of malcontents broke up, muttering to one another, and dispersed.

Gerald L. K. Smith's message, reiterating *The Protocols of the Elders of Zion,* was given when the European Jews accused of plotting America's downfall were themselves being herded into railroad cars and gassed in concentration camps. We didn't know much about that yet—the camps weren't liberated for another year. But I'd thought it commonly known that the Nazis were giving the Jews a hard time. These Americans were ready to do so too. A dangerous doctrine. Hard to accept that any sane person could believe such a farrago of lies and deceptions, as though Hitler had done nothing to provoke the war in Europe nor had the Japanese been the aggressors at Pearl Harbor. That Smith had a receptive audience here demonstrated the isolation, ignorance, and smoldering resentments of these farmers, who had no contact with the world beyond their own crops, pastures, and debts. A two-pint demagogue like Gerald L. K. Smith could sway this bunch of ignorant rubes—hadn't southern Ohio and Indiana been Ku Kluxer country in the twenties?—but could a smoother, more sophisticated politician rouse a larger rabble and sell such envy and hatred to the whole country? I'd read Sinclair Lewis's *It Can't Happen Here* and had to wonder. Negroes were still being lynched in the South, there had been race riots after the First World War. Who could tell what lay ahead?

This, fortunately, was not my only experience among Ohio farm people. The night before Thanksgiving I was having supper alone in the only restaurant in Yellow Springs. In the booth across from me was an elderly couple, obviously farming folk. I could tell they were studying me. Then the woman said something to her husband, and he spoke up: "Soldier, aren't you going home for Thanksgiving?" No, I said, I couldn't get enough time off to make the trip. "Well then, how would you like to have Thanksgiving dinner with us?" and on the back of a paper napkin he drew a map of how to reach their farm some twenty miles out in the country, down a one-lane dirt road till you turn right at a crossing just over the bridge . . .

Their farm was opulent; corncrakes filled to bursting, dozens of roosting hens, a pair of matched dray horses in the barn, and in the house a cheery fire in the parlor, a huge stove warming the kitchen. There, at a long table, assembled the whole family, all the men over forty, the women of like age except for one younger, and a little boy. These were the host's brothers and their wives, daughter-in-law and grandchild, and a hired man. I was treated as an honored guest, the surrogate for their son absent at a distant base. I felt as though I'd sat at the table in Whittier's "Snowbound." The dinner was a feast of plenty—a huge turkey, platters of succotash and boiled potatoes, home-brewed cider, steaming pumpkin pies, fragrant Ida Reds and Winesaps after dinner. Everything on the table they had grown right on the farm.

The next day I wrote them a letter of thanks, and when back at the Field sent their little grandson a scale model, no longer needed for a training film, of the B-25, the plane on which his father was a crewman.

★   ★   ★

Weekends were hard to get through, with no work to keep my mind off loneliness, for I had no girl. The Service Club in Dayton was for enlisted men, not officers, and I didn't want to hang around the Officers' Club at Patterson, an unlikely place to meet unattached women, but heavy odds that that's where Jean and her new captain would be of a Saturday night. Cincinnati had been our territory; in a spirit of masochism I returned there one weekend, to set out from Fountain Square alone. There was a secondhand bookshop nearby I'd noticed one time on our way to a concert, and now that time lay on my hands, I thought I'd explore it. And I made a very lucky strike—in a bin on the sidewalk, among many tattered paperbacks and discarded popular novels, a copy of *New Poems 1944,* edited by Oscar Williams. Three hundred pages of poems, many by men in the American and British services—even one Australian. And, at the back, photographs of the poets. A few I'd heard of—Auden, Cummings, Frost, Marianne Moore, Edith Sitwell in the first, non-combatant section. None of the soldier-poets in the second half of the book was known to me. Meeting their work would occupy many a long evening back in Yellow Springs.

New book under my arm, I walked on rather aimlessly. By now it was late afternoon. There was no breeze coming off the Ohio River, the streets were hot and dusty, and in a mindless daze I just kept my feet plodding one after the other. Snapping out of this reverie, I realized I was no longer on familiar ground—I'd wandered into the Negro section of the city. Black men in undershirts sat on stoops, some playing cards, some swigging bottles of wine. Loud, high-pitched, raucous laughter burst out of open windows. Women with their heads in bandannas swaggered along the sidewalk. Then this jangle of urban sounds and voices was suddenly pierced by the clear, pure notes of a trumpet, the opening bars of that evergreen standby "I've Found a New Baby" sailing out of the open door of a tavern on the corner, backed by a rhythm section and a high-pitched saxophone weaving, embroidering, riffing in and around the tune. I stood transfixed, for what could I be hearing but the inimitable Sidney Bechet!

I entered the tavern, where the only auditor of the band was a white-haired black man behind the bar. Evidently this was a warm-up session for that night's performance. I came to the bar, took a stool, and ordered a beer, but the bartender simply motioned me to shush, not drawing my glass until the number was over. It was indeed Sidney Bechet, whose swooping descents, sudden burstings into the lower register or soarings above the trumpet made an ever-shifting contrapuntal duet between the two melody instruments. But who was the trumpeter, playing mostly straight melody, his pure tone defining the themes Bechet elaborated? He was just a kid, looked about seventeen, and what's more, he was a white boy.

Between sets I met him. Johnny Windhurst was travelling with the maestro, apprenticing himself to Bechet. His presence in this group in a black tavern was quite extraordinary—jazz was by no means integrated in 1944. A few white Dixieland players recorded with black musicians—the pianist Art Hodes, the clarinettist Mezz Mezzrow; but jazzmen made their livings in nightclubs and at dances where racial mixing was not condoned. Only Benny Goodman, whose popularity made him impregnable, could get away with Teddy Wilson and, later, Lionel Hampton in his Trio, Quartet, and Sextet.

I spent an exhilarating hour listening to this little combo. Even before college I had bought a number of recordings by Bechet, and added more after the war, but I never heard Johnny Windhurst again. I believe he died young, perhaps was drafted and killed in the war. Had he survived and made recordings, he would, I believe, have become a jazz legend like Bix Beiderbecke or Bunny Berrigan, two great trumpeters prematurely dead.

That night, in my bare hotel room, I turned the pages of *New Poems 1944,* starting with the latter half of the book, "Poems from the Armed Forces." Here were poems unlike anything I'd ever read—Richard Eberhart (Lieutenant, U.S. Naval Reserve) writing:

> You would think the fury of aerial bombardment
> Would rouse God to relent . . .

concluding, after three stanzas rhetorically attacking man "No farther advanced than in his ancient furies," with this sudden change in tone:

> Of Van Wettering I speak, and Averill,
> Names on a list, whose faces I do not recall
> But they are gone to early death, who late in school
> Distinguished the belt feed lever from the belt holding pawl.

Then I came on John Manifold (Lieutenant, Australian Intelligence Corps) whose "Fife Tune (6/8) for 6 Platoon, 308th I.T.C." summoned "A twelve-year-old darling" who ran downstairs to see "the men flowing past her . . . Adoring her there":

> It's seldom I'll see
> A sweeter or prettier,
> I doubt we'll forget her
> In two years or three,
> And lucky he'll be
> She takes for a lover
> While we are far over
> The treacherous sea.

And Roy Fuller (Fleet Air Arm, Royal Navy), whose "January 1940," written at the height of the blitz of London, seemed a tract for such times, a reassurance that poetry was always wrung out of distress and suffering, that art could, indeed must, continue to be created in even the direst circumstances of the war:

> Swift had pains in his head.
> Johnson dying in bed
> Tapped the dropsy himself.

Blake saw a flea and an elf.
. . . .
Donne, alive in his shroud,
Shakespeare in the coil of a cloud,
Saw death very well as he
Came crab-wise and massy.
I envy not only their talents
And fertile lack of balance
But the appearance of choice
In their sad and fatal voice.

These were among the poems I soon had in memory, lines which have stayed with me for over half a century. From them I drew resolve to write of what was truly and deeply felt, an ambition much more easily defined than fulfilled. One could but keep trying.

★   ★   ★

Driving my flivver daily between Yellow Springs and Wright Field, I was using up my gas rations all too quickly. Joining a car pool seemed the solution. A married civilian in the Tech Data manuals unit, Jarvis Coullard, lived in Yellow Springs and told me he was in a pool with a couple of married civilians and a captain, and with Olga Corey, the daughter of an economics professor, who all had jobs at the Field. Now each had to drive only once a week, with a car full of friendly colleagues. By the end of the first week I asked Olga to a movie at the college, and picking her up at her parents' house, met them.

Only a college as unconventional as Antioch would have had on its faculty a professor as unconventional as Lewis Corey. Founded before the Civil War by Horace Mann, one of dozens of little colleges in Ohio villages, Antioch became distinctive during the Depression when Edwin Morgan, former head of the Tennessee Valley Administration, was its president. Applying New Deal pragmatism to education, Morgan devised a five-year curriculum in which students spent alternate terms studying on campus and away on jobs; wherever possible, these jobs were in fields related to their studies. Many advantages to this scheme. Employment was intended to help bright kids from impoverished families work their way through college, but by the war years the plan attracted bright kids from the unimpoverished middle class. The college could have twice the number of students enrolled as the number of rooms in its dorms, and the faculty could be kept small, since half the student body was always employed elsewhere, alternating terms with those in class. In time I hired two Antioch students—English majors—as editorial apprentices; they did proofreading and helped with layout.

In this college so devoted to utilitarian realities as well as to the humanities and sciences, economics was taught by a man with no college degrees—in fact he'd never finished high school—but with a most unusual background. Born Luigi Fraina in Italy, he had been brought to New York at the age of three when his father emigrated to escape persecution for republicanism. His mother could neither read nor write. They lived among fellow Italians on the Lower East Side. When he was fifteen his father died and the boy left school for good. As stated in his entry in the *Dictionary of American Biography* (on which I've relied for these details), "*The New York Journal* hired him as a cub reporter, and agnostic and socialist groups became his college." He must have been a quick study, for he was soon editor of the *New Review,* "then the theoretical voice of the left wing of the Socialist party." Briefly jailed for opposing U.S. entry in the First World War, "Fraina became what Theodore Draper described as the 'one man who led the way to a pro-Communist Left Wing.'" In 1917 he met Trotsky, Bukharin, and Kollontai, whose planned collaboration with him in editing *New International* was aborted by their departure for Russia on the eve of its Revolution. "During this period Fraina also edited *Modern Dance Magazine;* throughout his life he wrote on plays, poetry, novels, art, and music."

As national editor and international secretary of the Communist Party of America, Fraina was a delegate in 1920 to the Second Congress of the Communist International. "While there he was first falsely accused and then vindicated of being a police agent." In Moscow he met and married a woman employed by the Comintern, but by 1922 "he was out of the Communist movement, living in Mexico with his wife and newborn daughter." No doubt the accusations against him in Moscow, as well as the conspiratorial and denunciatory climate of factional revolutionary organizations, opened his eyes to the chasm between Communist premises and promises and the unlikelihood of their fulfillment. His independent mind, his background of readings so much broader than that of Party ideologues, made him reject the rigidity and intolerance of the C.P. line. From that day on he was reviled, slandered, and defamed by Communist propagandists; no one so dangerous to them as an informed apostate. He changed his name to Lewis Corey, not to escape this persecution—he fought back in articles, speeches, books—but to establish a new public identity. Henceforth he was an anti-Communist theorist, a Marxian economist devoted to democratic socialism. Active in the labor movement, in 1940 he helped to found the Union for Democratic Action, which soon became the popular movement Americans for Democratic Action. His next post, in 1942, was at Antioch.

How could even so liberal a college as Antioch add to its faculty a man with such a résumé? It must be recalled that Corey's fame was based on his book *The Decline of American Capitalism* (1934), a 600-page work of serious scholarship, widely praised, and by his prominence in the liberal A.D.A., the aims of which were consonant with those of Morgan's college. Corey's earlier radicalism must have seemed irrelevant to his present commitment to finding rational solutions to poverty and the maldistribution of wealth. He took from Marx analysis of the injustices and weaknesses of capitalism, and also the part of Marx's thought the Party ignored and subverted, the humanism on which his critique was based. Corey was an anomaly in American political life, a self-educated, European-style social democrat who joined to his economic-political thought a deep involvement with and loyalty to the arts in Western culture.

He was a wiry little man, whom the actor playing Louis Fraina in the movie *Reds* did not at all resemble. Corey would sit on a folding chair under the shade trees on his lawn across the street from the campus, a week's *New York Times* at his feet, a pair of library shears a foot long in hand, as he sliced out articles bearing on his teaching or research. Behind wire-rimmed spectacles his black eyes darted. He spoke in a rush of enthusiasm, a passionate commitment.

Corey's wife, Esther, was a Russian earth mother whose warmth embraced and consoled many a freshman away from home for the first time. Students came and went in the Corey household, an oasis of friendliness. Soon I came and went there too, for I was seeing Olga frequently and talking much with her parents. Lewis Corey was a natural teacher, and in me he found a willing auditor. I, who couldn't handle my Columbia economics course, with its mathematical representations of supply and demand, was fascinated by Corey's demonstrations of how economic policies both were based on and influenced politics as well as determining the quality of life of each nation's people. The calls of Communism to world revolution Corey had long since dismissed, rejecting its insistence on historical necessity to describe what his observation and experience proved impossible. What was possible was reform, democratically achieved.

His Marxist analysis was revelatory. I had never encountered a mind like his. My father, a product of the booming twenties, despite having lost almost all he owned in the Depression and his none-too-successful struggles to keep afloat since then, continued to believe in the largesse of the market. He, like my mother, was a sentimental New Deal Democrat. Perhaps they realized that FDR had saved capitalism by blunting its unregulated inhumanity, putting across as much as he cannily knew the American people and their Congress would take of the Socialist platform on which Norman Thomas had gained a million votes a few years before. But mild endorsement of government regulatory bodies was not the same as Corey's radical attacks on capitalism's remaining flaws.

Intellectual stimulation was combined with the Coreys' accepting me as a member of their circle, a most welcome embrace by a family whose warmth and coherence so differed from the home life I had had. Some years later I had occasion to write what Corey had meant to me.

I N   M E M O R Y   O F   L E W I S   C O R E Y

I

He knew I'd never be a true disciple
When I coughed, embarrassed by his love
For Swinburne. Then, I thought
A real reformer ought
To praise revolt in *everything*.
But he'd no use for verse that didn't 'sing.'
And so he taught
(I didn't know it for a lesson yet)
That poetry and politics
Don't mix
In simple rhetorics.
You can see
How young I was, how out of fashion he.
I since have read of Fraina in a book,
How Madison Square Garden rose and shook
At his command, ten thousand voices one
Vowing to free
From imperialist invasion
Archangel far across the sea.
But what's all that to me?
I wasn't even born when Fraina led
His fractious splinter in those Red
Matchstick plays at power.
The man I honor is the man I knew:
Self-purged before the Moscow Trials,
He came through
The withering away, as at the stake,
Of every vow his fervent youth could make
But one, and that the most romantic trust
That shown the injustice of our institutions,
We will choose to make them just.

Corey had long done with revolutions,
But I confess, I haven't found mankind
As sensible as he to what enlightened mind
Describes as the common good

To a self-seeking multitude.
It's fifteen years he's dead now, yet the thought
Of Corey makes my mind rehearse
All that he taught,
And this thought chides—
How little else have I reformed, besides
The diction of my verse;
Should the commonwealth, like art, seek perfect
forms
What can it learn from my self-searching trade?
Those were the images he made,
Those, and the image of a man possessed
By reason to persuade
A race spoon-fed upon self-interest
To set the table, break its hoarded bread.
What can I do with his bequest
Who wished no man to suffer wrong,
But make his memory a song?

And I did. But I didn't reprint this elegy in my selected poems because the "song" proved, years later, too topical for comprehension, its tune and rhythm too heavily borrowed from Yeats.

Corey returned to educational work in the labor movement in 1951. By then, with the cold war in full swing, American politics had turned to the extreme right in ugly ways as hysterical fears of Communism were fed by ambitious politicians. Corey was investigated by the F.B.I. and was threatened with deportation under the McCarran Act. A paid informer, Harvey Matusow, later convicted of perjury for his testimony, accused Corey as a Communist subversive to a congressional committee and a press unwilling and unable to distinguish between Party ideology and anti-Communist Marxism. Against this charge effective defense was impossible. Corey attacked capitalism, so wasn't his claim of opposing the Party just a clever smokescreen to hide his Communist subversion? The spirit of McCarthyism had infected public discourse.

How far Corey had come from the Communism of his youth can be inferred from a passage typical of his thought. It's the concluding paragraph of his contribution to a symposium, "Which Way for the Middle Class?" in the issue of the *Antioch Review* (Spring 1945) in which my article on jazz appeared. Corey wrote:

> The middle class was the great architect of political democracy; it can become an architect of supplementary economic democracy. In any event the middle class will be a crucial factor in coming social changes. Without the co-operative understanding and action of progressive middle class, workers, and farmers, there can be no peaceful change for a new society which will broaden and deepen democratic procedures and values. (87)

A man with convictions such as these scarcely seems an enemy of the American republic.

Corey's deportation order arrived on Christmas Eve, 1952. He was fired by the union for which he was educational director. In September 1953 the anguish of this persecution by the government brought on the heart attack and cerebral hemorrhage that killed him. My "song" went like this:

II

It was a time that cowardice
Begat upon disgrace;
What else had numbed all decent sense
In so many in high place,
While those whom popular hatred fed
Rose up by being base?
　　　　　　—As we may remember.

They tarred him with black printer's ink,
They smeared him in the town,
They bought a hireling liar
To cry his good name down.
But what can harm his spirit now?
He's gone to his renown.
　　　　　　—As we may remember.

For he's an honored citizen
In the republic of the dead,
And we who were his countrymen
—Now let the truth be said—
May learn to cut our plenty's loaf
    With his blessing on our bread.

At his death, Corey was researching a biography of the nine-teenth-century women's rights reformer and companion of the Marquis de Lafayette, Fanny Wright. His last article appeared in *The New Leader* the week he died, an appreciation of the poetry of Heinrich Heine.

This man's daughter combined her father's political passion with her mother's rounded womanliness. She was an adept of what to me were many mysteries, her conversation sprinkled with aphorisms derived from factional struggles of which I was hearing for the first time, such as the rejoinder by a Party member to the deviationist who deserted with his small band of acolytes—"All right, Schactman, we'll seize power without you!" Laughingly, she acknowledged the futility of such grandiose illusions. Her own politics was a romantic, total commitment to her father's causes. Olga, I gathered, had been on the barricades at Queens College to wrest control of the student government from members of the Young Communist League. At the same time she was a voracious reader of the latest novels, on which she held pronounced opinions. She was, I learned after a time, married to a merchant seaman (of course an active anti-Communist in the National Maritime Union), but, twenty years before the rise of feminism, kept her own name.

Olga I thought sophisticated, not only in left-wing politics but in life itself, truly a woman of the world. I took her to be so mature, she must be older than myself; years later, looking up her father in the biographical reference work I've summarized above, I was surprised to discover that her birth and mine were separated by at most a year. Knowing her and her parents gave me experience of a close and supportive family and an exposure to reformist politics I'd not otherwise have had.

★ ★ ★

The *Digest* staff now numbered a dozen, half military, half civilian. Miss Leane had retired; her place as head civilian was filled by H. Lee Jones. He was a handsome white-haired man who bore himself with dignity; had been, he told me, on the psychology faculty for six years at Ohio State, then a journalist, was a professional photographer, and a Unitarian minister. Not until much later did I understand that the six-year appointment at O.S.U. indicated failure to be tenured. Was Lee an unusually adaptable man of many talents, or did his checkered career as jack-of-all-trades indicate something else? In any case, he was immediately able to take hold of his responsibilities with us, and since the staff had traditionally been headed by a civil servant, now in tandem with me as officer in charge, we had to get along. I reckon Lee Jones must have been in his mid or late fifties at this time, at least as old as my father, but we managed good teamwork. We got to know one another better when we were sent on detached service to put our combined expertise into rescuing a disastrous manual on Materiel Command procedures that had been ill written in Wichita, where we were snowbound by a blizzard for a good ten days.

Now, among others on the staff, we had another secretary, Lucille; Joanne Whipple, an Antioch student at work as editorial trainee; Pfc. Macauley, nicotine-stained, intensely conscientious, a former advertising writer from a small Michigan city; Sgt. Sidney Botvinick, an enthusiastic New Yorker; Jim, 4-F because of a collapsed lung, from nearby Hamilton, where he, who yearned for intellectual stimulation, felt as out of place as did the young man in Sherwood Anderson's *Winesburg, Ohio;* and a corporal, Jack, a seasoned ex-sports reporter from the *New York Daily Mirror.*

Jack had not been out of place on that tabloid, for he had a tabloid outlook on life, but even at this benign post he was certainly out of his element in the Army. He was older than the rest of the servicemen, a last resort of his draft board, at the maximum age for induction. Coming late into the Army, he didn't take it seriously. He spent as much time as possible in Dayton,

including hours when he should have been on details up on the
hill. He took to turning up mornings at his desk late, bleary-
eyed, unshaven, nor was he prudently secretive about it. In fact
he bragged that he had him a woman in town, a great lay, a wild
one, more fun than any woman he'd ever known in New York.
She was a mountain gal from Kentucky, could hold her booze as
well as he—and that was going some; never knew any broad like
her before. His style, combining dissolute indiscipline with brag-
gadocio, did not endear him to the rest of us; indeed, everyone
thought him a bad egg, an object of curiosity since we all knew
he was heading for a big downfall—when and what would it be?
Jack was no great help on my staff, but then, he didn't last long.

One morning he didn't turn up at all. Around ten o'clock I
had a caller: a detective from the Dayton police force. He interviewed me for what little I could tell him of Jack's habits and
proclivities, for I'd only recently learned the name of his woman.
The detective told me what he could about the reason for Jack's
absence that morning. I sent him up the hill to see the C.O. of
the barracks Jack had occupied as rarely as possible. Soon the
whole Field knew what had happened. It was a classic tale. Were
the full story known back in the mountain town from which
Jack's woman had come, wouldn't this tale be put into an appropriate form and set to music by some old fellow with whiskers
and a banjo? His tune, with its chords and riffs, would redeem
the banality of the words and theme. At my office desk I typed
out these lines:

> I'll tell you the story of Lillie Mae Hartley.
> Some's all true, and some but partly.
>
> Got to admit, Lillie had a way with her,
> And few was the men smart enough to play with her.
>
> When Lil took a lover, she made one demand,
> On no other woman can he lay a hand.
>
> Lil took a lover, name of Corporal Jack.
> He never should have cheated behind her back.

When Jack didn't show, Lil got the blues,
To console herself, drank a bottle of booze.

Jack came in late, cheap scent filled the room,
Only trouble was, it warn't Lil's perfume.

Took off his shirt, had a smudge on the collar,
Sure looked like lipstick, but not Lil's color.

—Darlin', she said, tell me where you been,
And while telling me that, say who you've seen.

—I sure love you, Lil, but you don't got to know
Everyone I see, or everywhere I go.

They found him at midnight, on her kitchen floor,
And Lil was just standin there, leanin on the door,

Holdin her gun—it was even smokin.
Looks like they got her now, ain't no jokin.

So Lillie Mae was arrested, charged, and held for trial. That
got quite a play in the local paper. In view of how it came out, I
added some couplets to my ballad:

The court was so quiet when Lillie Mae arose
You could have heard a flea blowin his nose.

She smiled at the judge and told of the wrong
Done to her virtue. She didn't speak long,

But whenever Judge looked at her, and that warn't
    seldom,
She gives him her smile, an maybe she spelled him.

So they set her free as a cloud to go
Except in Dayton her face she mustn't show.

Some say she's in Virginia, some say Kentucky,
But you've got to agree, Lillie sure was lucky.

Corporal Jack was a casualty it was hard to mourn—we scarcely knew him, he met the fate he'd courted, and we'd remember him for that. My ballad I passed around to the late Jack's colleagues but have shown it to no one else until now.

Jack's death left us a bit shorthanded, not that he had done anything like his share of abstracting. What bothered me was that this staff was really unqualified to deal with the increasingly advanced technical literature we had to cover. By now we were receiving preprints of papers to be given at the meetings of the major engineering societies, and the fields covered had grown. Development of new aircraft, new gunsights, new bombs, new bombsights, new instruments was being reported in the publications we received and were to abstract for the *Digest's* readers. I tried to condense several papers on meteorology—weather forecasting had been added to the list of concerns we had to cover—but couldn't understand them. I'd met the Antioch professor of astronomy, Lawrence Lafleur, and on a hunch brought two of the articles to Yellow Springs to show to him. He, serendipitously, turned out to be an amateur meteorologist and volunteered to write up the abstracts.

In conversation while walking across the Antioch campus with Lafleur and Gwilym Owen, the head of the physics department, I said that Army Classification was sending us ex-advertising copywriters and broken-down newspaper hacks to work on scientific literature. Owen said, "You really ought to see Dr. Patterson. He's retired now and lives in Xenia—he was vice president of the college and a distinguished chemist. For years he was the editor of *Chemical Abstracts,* which does for chemistry what your magazine is trying to do for aviation."

What a great idea! And how obvious—why hadn't I, why hadn't any of the officers before and above me in Technical Information ever thought that, instead of making do with amateurs, the Air Force should consult an editor or two of similar civilian projects in the sciences, to see how the work should be done? I had never heard of *Chemical Abstracts*. In truth I was un-aware that the professional society in any of the hard sciences published a review of research. To be fair to my predecessors and superiors, *The Technical Data Digest* was but one of their numer-ous responsibilities. None was a scientist, nor had they found un-satisfactory the way the *Digest* had limped along; how could they have known that? And besides, they had more important projects to administer.

I wrote Dr. Austin Patterson on Air Force letterhead and soon received his invitation to call at his home in Xenia. He was a tall, slender man who carried his years well and resembled a country doctor. I passed through the glassed-in porch of his frame house and we sat in his parlor. His wife poured tea while he explained how *Chemical Abstracts* covered thousands of articles a year from the world over, with the help of chemists on university and col-lege faculties and on the staffs of industries, who were sent the materials to be summarized. He suggested that I go to Colum-bus to visit the staff at the headquarters of the American Chem-ical Society, on the Ohio State University campus.

When I reported all this to Colonel Davis, he immediately agreed. So I was assigned to detached service and spent several days in Columbus, fifty miles away. The editor, Dr. E. S. Crane, and his staff on *Chemical Abstracts* shared their methods, showed me the files identifying potential abstractors and yet other files recording the work done by each, and the in-house editorial procedures after receipt of these contributions. I came back to Dayton with a good grasp of how to organize a more profes-sional staff of abstractors. All that was required was to recruit them—from universities, from industries.

And, Colonel Davis added, to pay them, for the Air Force had to have contractual arrangements with any persons, firms, or in-stitutions that provided services, contracts involving payment. I'd have to initiate a contract for Professor Lafleur, whose work on the two meteorological abstracts would require that he be signed up as a consultant and paid. This entanglement in red tape could wait, however, until we had lined up additional contributors.

Colonel Davis now proposed that he and I go together on a recruitment mission to Pittsburgh, starting with his old firm,

Gulf Oil, in whose subsidiary, Gulf Research and Development Company, were several Ph.D.s working on the development of aviation fuel and other military projects. He must have felt it would be advantageous to turn up with a military project for which the firm could provide the assistance of his former colleagues. In fact they were welcoming, and several agreed to become contributing abstractors.

The success of this little mission persuaded Colonel Davis to set me loose on my own, so after preparatory correspondence I was launched during April 1945 on detached service, a trip to M.I.T., Harvard, Yale, Columbia, Brooklyn Poly, N.Y.U., and Cooper Union to recruit abstractors. Not all of these schools were on my original itinerary, but some *Digest* recruits suggested colleagues at other institutions in their own or adjacent fields. For instance, at M.I.T., Professor Eric Reissner told me that his father, Hans, a mathematician at Brooklyn Polytechnic, would want to help. The elder Reissner, a refugee from Germany, was indeed glad to take on this very slight contribution to defeating Hitler. I also called in at the Society of Automotive Engineers and the American Society of Mechanical Engineers to ensure that preprints of papers to be given at their meetings be sent to the *Digest*.

I kept no notes of these meetings with deans and department heads but well recall that at both M.I.T. and Harvard the deans of the engineering schools, on questioning me about my own background, being well aware of the Columbia humanities requirements, emphasized their hope of reforming engineering education after the war by the inclusion of required study of literature, philosophy, and history. Their premise was that technical training alone was inadequate to prepare for the technological revolution ahead; humanistic study would help their graduates achieve intelligent leadership, dealing with the social consequences of technology, understanding better the full range of culture. This struck me as enlightened policy. Some twenty-five years later I had occasion to reflect on those conversations when reading an eloquently contrarian memoir, *At the Edge of History: Speculations on the Transformation of Culture* (1971), in which William Irwin Thompson condemns M.I.T (where he had taught Humanities in the 1960s) as "a power-mad institution dedicated to the opposites of humanistic values." Among other indictments, Thompson claimed that M.I.T. needed "a large psychiatric clinic because the effect of technological training is to do to the psyche what industry does to the environment. . . . Operating with a strictly logical and mechanistic model of the self, M.I.T. training reduces the self's truly complex nature to a few relatively standard industrial functions" (68, 75). Whether these are deserved rebukes to a major educator of technocrats I am not in a position to say, but Thompson's strictures suggest that the addition or inclusion of some humanities courses to a technical education might not have sufficient specific gravity to counterbalance the rest of the curriculum.

At Columbia my port of call was a building well known to me, the School of Engineering, and my first interview was with Dean Hinckley, who when we last met had welcomed my abandonment of engineering studies. Now he greeted me warmly, and wryly commented that it was so good to see an ex-student doing something so worthwhile for the war effort. Most of his alumni, he said, identifying themselves to Army Placement as students of engineering, had therefore been assigned to the Army Corps of Engineers, where they dug ditches, repaired roads, and swept runways. Army Classification, usually so incapable of matching men's training with military needs, seemed designed for its own incompetence. Hinckley then suggested the members of his faculty I should see—Professors Ettore A. Peretti and Victor Scottron—who were glad to be enlisted for occasional abstracting, lending the *Digest* their expertise in, respectively, metallurgy and aerodynamics.

By the end of my journey some thirty-five professors of engineering, physics, and other sciences, as well as researchers from several institutions additional to those already mentioned—Pittsburgh, George Washington, Ohio State, and Catholic Universities—had signed on. So had staff members from the Franklin Institute, the National Bureau of Standards, R. C. Mahon Company, and the National Lumbermen's Association (it may not be remembered that several aircraft and military gliders had molded-plywood fuselages). Now we could with confidence publish abstracts of ever-more-difficult scientific literature; but there were still many other articles, not as technically demanding, which the resident staff in Dayton abstracted as before.

In the course of this trip by train, I looked out the window of my Pullman compartment early one morning and noticed in village after village, as we sped through our own clouds of smoke, that the flags on every town hall were at half staff. Not until I got off the train did I learn that during the preceding night President Roosevelt had died. A whole day of seeing flags at half mast was a memorable image of the nation's shock and grief.

★   ★   ★

Now with a cadre of distinguished scientists ready to write those abstracts, I was raring to put them to work. Relying on the monthly checklist of topics from the heads of our laboratories, the staff in the office would choose the articles and papers to be sent to the contributors. For most journals, we'd give them the titles and page references to the relevant articles—they or their institutions were subscribers; we'd send duplicate copies of engineering society preprints, and the more arcane foreign materials we'd photostat for the abstractors.

"Whoa there," Colonel Davis cautioned. "First we have to process their contracts." Yes, I'd all but forgotten—the Air Force accepts no volunteerism; the government requires legal commitment, the exchange of money for services.

"But how much should we pay them? You know they're eager to do the work for nothing."

"How about fifteen dollars per column in the magazine?" Colonel Davis proposed. That looked to be enough to satisfy regulations, but so small an amount there'd be no budgetary difficulties. And the contributors would recognize that it was merely a token, no measure of their worth. A lawyer-in-uniform in Legal Affairs drafted the agreement. This was reproduced thirty-five times, with each contributor's name typed in. When I learned that these minuscule agreements would have to be processed in the very same way as million-dollar contracts for a new gunsight or a modified engine, and the wending of the papers through many stations of bureaucracy could take weeks, even months, I determined to walk them through myself.

In a chamber as large as a hangar, row on row of desks; at each a man in uniform who, when in civvies, had been an attorney, an insurance adjuster, an accountant, a tax inspector. In this army of bureaucrats each had on his desk a set of regulations several inches thick, to be consulted for the verification and validation of every paragraph of every document for whose perusal he was responsible. I spent nearly a week in this stifling military compound, resolutely moving my pile of papers from one officer's desk to the next, claiming that the pressure of publication deadlines made imperative their immediate attention to the abstractors' contracts. At last all were cleared, and our work could begin.

★　★　★

Major Ross had thought the colonels who headed the labs would be reluctant to spare their experts to write new articles for the *Digest,* but in fact they soon regarded such publication, reaching over 5,500 readers, some of them highly placed in the Air Force, as very desirable publicity for their individual units. When a new issue of the *Digest* rolled off the press each month, I made sure to present the first copies to Colonel Davis, one for his own file, others for him to send to the colonel whose subordinate officer had contributed the featured article.

So when the April–May 1945 issue came out (I can't recall why this was a double number), I brought copies to my C.O. "Looks like another handsome issue," he said, regarding the cover photograph of a technician testing a huge 110-inch wheel. "What's new this time?" Then he turned to the feature, and exploded, *"What the hell is this?* Here's an article on a jet engine, and it has the author identified as *in the Propeller Lab!"*

My heart sank. In one fell swoop a single misprint would humiliate Colonels Davis and Hayward and antagonize at least two other colonels: the one in charge of the Propeller Lab and the one over in Power Plant who'd not be pleased to have his man's work misattributed to a rival unit. And the error would hold up to ridicule the entire Technical Data Laboratory. "Who's responsible for this?"

I thought back a couple of nights, when several of the staff had stayed very late to finish layout and final proofreading so the dummy could be delivered to the printing plant first thing the next morning. The feature article, "A Method for Estimating Gas Turbine-Jet Airplane Performance," by Captain R. E. Hage, was one of the most technical essays we ever published, studded with graphs, charts, diagrams, and many mathematical equations—it was those that compelled the attention of the *Digest*'s proofreaders. No mistake could be made in them. The error must have slipped through when my hard-working crew were groggy with fatigue. Nor had it caught my eye. Already standing at attention, I straightened up to rigidity and said, "Sir, the responsibility is mine."

Then I had an idea. "Colonel, I know a print shop in Dayton with a sign in its window that says they can make rubber stamps to order in an hour. I can get several stamps, each with a black bar to cross out 'Propeller Lab,' and on the line below the bar, in italics say 'Power Plant Laboratory.' I'll see to it that every single copy is hand-stamped with this correction before it leaves the printing plant."

That somewhat mollified the colonel. I rushed to town to order a handful of customized stamps, then hurried back with them and several ink pads in hand, and asked Sgt. Botvinick, Pfc. Macauley, and Joanne, our Antioch intern, to stay late. We picked up sandwiches from the food vendor on the flight line, then went to the printing plant and one by one hand-stamped each copy, each of the over five thousand copies, of our magazine, far into the night. I had called Antioch College to explain why Joanne would be out very late. When, bleary-eyed, at last we completed our task, Macauley left to climb the hill to his barracks and we trudged to the parking lot—Sid Botvinick, who had his wife in Dayton, to join her, while I drove Joanne to her Antioch dorm. A few blocks away I flopped across my own bed without taking off my uniform, and three hours later was wrenched from sleep by the alarm clock. Back to the field I drove, not at all good for another day's work. I gave copies of the hand-corrected issues to Colonel Davis's assistant, then tried to prop my eyes open at my own desk.

An hour later Colonel Davis stopped by. "That's a very good issue this month," he said and moved on. I was left to infer that the grievous error of the misattributed article would not be mentioned again. Also in that issue was a full-page portrait of President Roosevelt, with a tribute to his leadership.

IV

ONLY a few months after *The Technical Data Digest,* with its distinguished contributors, was functioning on a really professional basis, the atom bomb was dropped and the war was over. Like the American jet fighter planes, this advanced model of the *TDD* was developed too late for optimum use in wartime.

Now the helium swiftly ran out of many balloons. Personal commitment to duty quickly eroded into calculation of points earned toward discharge, points awarded for months of service, more points for service overseas, still more for having been in a combat zone. The urgency of projects suddenly evaporated. With no war to win, motivation faded; men went to their assignments impatiently, did them dutifully, without enthusiasm. These changes of mood affected the Technical Data Branch no less than elsewhere in HQ Materiel Command.

There was much shuffling of personnel now. As those with enough points were released, their places were taken by newcomers. Captain Robert L. Chapman turned up in Tech Information, the only man who ever in the whole outfit had a literary sensibility, and a welcome companion he was to me. After the war he wrote a fine novel, I think never published, about a veteran's difficulties adjusting to civilian life.

We continued to prepare monthly issues of the *Digest,* rationalizing that, war or no war, the Air Force had to keep up with the latest technology. But from higher echelons came a new concern: would Congress continue to fund the Air Force as before? And if, as was almost certain, not, wouldn't the support functions of Air Technical Service Command be the first to fall to the axe, and Tech Information be among its first casualties? I spent much of September 1945 preparing a long memorandum, "Recommended Policy for Continuing The TECHNICAL DATA DIGEST During the Interim and Post-War Periods." My signature was followed by those of the approving higher-ups: Lt. Col. Woods, Chief Analysis Officer; Colonel D. L. Putt, Deputy Commanding General; and H. G. Knerr, U.S.A., Commanding.

Despite all this brass polish, the recommendation was disregarded. With Congress eager to reduce military spending, the Air Force suspended all its publications. Another memo followed, prepared by hands higher than mine, dated 3 December 1945, addressed to Commanding General, Army Air Forces, Attention: Air Adjutant General. This one was signed only by Major General Knerr, who the year before had been in England in charge of the huge supply and maintenance system supporting the Eighth Air Force, and whose endorsement, as a commander who best knew the needs of the Air Force, might be expected to carry weight. The memorandum was titled "Reestablishment of the AAF Publication The TECHNICAL DATA DIGEST." The grounds now included the magazine's role in fulfilling a presidential executive order, since it "offers the AAF the most economical and efficient medium for . . . the free and general dissemination of enemy scientific and industrial information." The Air Documents Division, Intelligence, was "cataloging and translating approximately 500,000 such enemy documents from the European theater alone." (One set I remember seeing comprised long interviews with Luftwaffe pilots who analyzed the combat characteristics of each of the Allied aircraft.) Many advantages would accrue from publication, as attested by unsolicited letters appended from aircraft companies, universities, the U.S. Navy Bureau of Aeronautics, etc. And it would cost only $27,500 to print not more than 8,000 copies per month.

All to no avail. The *Digest* was killed. A friend in our art department drew a cartoon showing the ghost of the *TDD* hovering over its own tombstone inscribed with the dates of its life (1930–1945) and the legend "R.I.P." All members of the *Digest* staff signed this memorial to our work.

It must have been in an effort to secure congressional support that HQ Materiel Command played host to a delegation of members of Congress. They were to tour the Field, to be given opportunities to see how important it was for national security that our functions be adequately funded. I was called in by Colonel Davis, who told me that, as the most junior officer in the Branch, I was assigned to escort the visiting congressmen, to guide them through two exhibits: the B-10 and an experimental German rocket interceptor.

Down on the flight line for the past few days there had been a huge aircraft whose tail towered far above the intervening buildings. This was the B-10, a prewar precursor of the much sleeker, smaller B-17. The B-10's huge engines and propellers could make it lumber along at 200 mph. There were tunnels in the wings so the flight engineer could crawl from the fuselage to any of the four engine nacelles. The point of showing this behemoth to the congressmen was to demonstrate how commitment to research in every aspect of aeronautical design led to the great improvements in the B-17; were it not for government-funded developmental research, we would have had to wage the war with slow, vulnerable, ungainly bombers. If the USAAF was to keep its hegemony in the postwar world, similar progress would be necessary in the future.

Exhibit B demonstrated the same point by opposite evidence, the Nazis' last weapon of desperation. One was on display outside the Tech Information building. It resembled two metallic barrels hooped together with stubby wings protruding. There was a transparent canopy over the pilot's seat in the middle of the thing, but it had no landing gear. In the rear half were the rockets that powered it, and forward of the pilot, two dozen rockets that he could launch individually, in pairs, threes, fours, sixes, a dozen at a time, or all at once. This craft was intended to decimate formations of B-17s, B-25s, and British Lancasters. Its tiny size made it able to weave among Allied bomber formations and avoid being shot down by defending fighter planes.

To get up to an altitude of some 35,000 feet, the rocket plane, with pilot inside, was launched by being stood up vertically on the ground, the engine started by exterior ignition—a man on the ground attached a battery and flipped a switch—and it would whoosh up into the upper atmosphere. This sudden acceleration would leave the pilot momentarily unconscious; the craft would automatically level off at the desired altitude, the pilot would come to and seek out the Allied bombers. All he had to do was steer the thing and fire the rockets. His rockets discharged, he would use up all his fuel flying back over German-held territory, then press a lever that ejected him into space and divided the craft in half, the spent rocket launcher tumbling earthward. Two parachutes opened: from one dangled the propulsor rockets, to be retrieved and used again; descending from the other, the pilot would also be retrieved for use on the next mission.

I remembered this piece of devilish ingenuity as the "Nadir"; only in preparing this book did I learn, from a Web site devoted to military aviation history, the actual name: it was the Bachem Ba 349 Natter. Obviously someone had Anglicized the pronunciation of the German word, which means "viper." (My recollections of the Natter were accurate except that it proved one and a half times longer, at 6.1 meters, than I'd remembered.)

To so bizarre a weapon were the Nazis reduced when Allied bombings, advancing armies, and the pressure of time made impossible further development of conventional aircraft. They could but concoct a suicidal contraption which, now that one had been captured and shipped to Wright Field, the Air Force couldn't get anyone to fly. Neither American nor captured Luftwaffe pilots would undertake such a mission. So the weapon remained untested by us—we didn't even know if it had ever actually flown in combat, for there were no reported sightings. After fifty-five years, I learned that of the twenty that were built, only one was flown, and it disintegrated in midair, killing its pilot.

From these exhibits the congressmen were invited to draw the inevitable conclusion about the essentiality of continued research and development. There had been distrust of our Soviet allies all along; now perhaps that would translate into continuing support for the Air Force.

★ ★ ★

As the most junior Tech Information officer, I was given one more assignment apart from my usual duties. I was to be sent to Washington, carrying an attaché case containing the top-secret papers devised by the world-renowned Hungarian-born mathematician Theodore von Karman. I would accompany Dr. von Karman to the Pentagon, where I'd deliver his research, and then return to Wright Field. And what was this secret research about? Since von Karman was director of the Jet Propulsion Laboratory, chief consultant and founder of Aerojet Engineering, not to mention chairman of the Scientific Advisory Board to the Chief of Staff, USAAF, one could speculate on what he was working.

Was it possible that I was chosen to be his guide, courier, and companion because he had seen my article in the *Digest* a year before? Of course not, that was merely a summary of research then in the public domain. No, it was my juniority in Tech Information that gave me this free ride to the Pentagon. Professor von Karman, I was informed, held the simulated rank of major general, so that in case of his capture by the enemy he would be extended the courtesies appropriate to a prisoner of that high rank.

Thus it was that a youth who couldn't pass college calculus was courier for the greatest mathematician on the Allied side, perhaps in the world. When I reported for duty, a major, until then the custodian of the sacred case, not only handed it over, he slipped a manacle on my wrist, to which was attached a foot-long chain. The other end was secured to the case. He gave me the key with strict orders that I was not to separate myself from cuff, chain, and case until I had delivered the top-secret documents to the designated recipient in the Pentagon. Feeling in part like a convict, I grasped the handle of the attaché case, hoping no one would notice the chain, and tried to conceal the manacle under the cuff of my jacket. I was then driven in a jeep to the flight line, where, arriving in an Army sedan, von Karman followed me, climbing the ladder into the plane. We spoke little—he during the flight made further calculations in a notebook which should by all rights have been secured as were those I was carrying. He was a slight, elderly man resembling a befuddled professor who, setting out to the newsstand to buy the latest paper, forgets the point of his errand and returns with a Hershey bar instead. On our day trip I had to make all the practical arrangements. I can't remember any of whatever conversation he had with me, just have kept the impression of a kindly, grandfatherly man utterly without any pretensions.

At the Pentagon the problem was to find the designated office. A captain guided us through endless passages—the building itself seemed the embodiment of bureaucracy, its architectural design red tape made physically manifest in three dimensions. At last we reached the office, where a major general welcomed von Karman and his adjutant looked to me to unlock my manacle and turn over the case of calculations. Mission accomplished, I was flown back to Wright Field.

★ ★ ★

Antioch College was filling up with discharged veterans, men who had been in combat in Europe or the Pacific islands. It was inevitable to compare their experiences, and those of my college friends with whom I'd kept in touch, with my own three years in the Zone of the Interior. None of my closest friends would return to Columbia. My roommate Stan had been wounded in the Pacific Theater; recuperating at an Army hospital in California, when discharged he finished college at U.C.L.A. Sid Lamb, from Montreal, had joined the Canadian infantry and gone ashore in Normandy; after the war he went to McGill. Barney de Jarnett had acted on the romantic impulse of his southern background and, as though volunteering in 1861, joined the cavalry. What use men on horseback would have been against the Japanese was hard to imagine; Barney and his mount were drowned in a training accident, an attempted landing exercise in rough waters off New Zealand.

Many college men had been called from Enlisted Reserve just in time for the Battle of the Bulge. Veterans I knew or met had spent months in foxholes dodging enemy shells; had sweated out tropical diseases and faced rifle fire and bursting shells on Asiatic islands. Others had ridden in tanks through blasted cities in France and Germany; had been dropped behind enemy lines as saboteurs or gatherers of intelligence; had liberated starving Jews from concentration camps; had exchanged fire with enemy warships. Still others had flown through flak and enemy fighters or survived from torpedoed ships. Some had been wounded.

While they were having their mettle and manhood tested in these terrible circumstances, seeing men blown to pieces, luckily surviving the deaths of comrades, I had held a desk job in Ohio. I'd heard of the guilt felt by those who survived battles in which their buddies had died. Inevitably, a portion of guilt attached to my thoughts of how I'd been untested, untoughened, and unscathed. I felt the need to justify, if only to myself, my assignment, convince myself—as had my civilian colleagues at the Jordanoff Company four years before—that what I had done, too, had a part, however slight, in winning the war. Was what I had done as useful as what I might have been ordered and, perhaps, been able to do, had I, like these veterans, been in a combat unit? Perhaps as a rifleman or a fighter pilot I'd have had little or no effect on the outcome of battle. There was of course no way to know. I could not help but feel that my service in the Zone of the Interior had kept me from initiation into a maturity shared by some of my friends and many of my generation. There was a certain spiritual space between those who had been under fire, had seen men killed, had had to kill enemies, had tasted fear and survived, and those who had no such experiences. Not that many talked much about the war—those with bad memories tried to get back into civilian life as best they could; veterans of the Zone of the Interior were not tempted to talk much either.

While my assignment to Wright Field was, to my mind, a rational Army decision to use to best advantage my specialized experience, from another point of view I'd also been a pawn in the power plays of various superior officers. The colonel who had urged and helped me be assigned to Materiel Command—that made him, posted to New York City, look good to his general at Wright Field. Even my mere presence there could be used to advantage; I received my final promotion from a new lieutenant colonel in charge of our unit—his name has not remained on memory's scroll, but I do recall he was directly commissioned from an advertising career and had brought to the Air Force his great innovation in that business, so the AAF could win the war with Day-Glo. He'd been at his new post only a week, had no idea what I did or how well or ill I did it, when he summoned me to his office and returned my salute with the comment, "I'm putting you in for first lieutenant. I want to command *men*, not shavetails!" Of course he was the one bucking for promotion, sure he could get those eagles on his collar if he had more men in higher ranks under him. My promotion came through, though hardly as recognition for duties well done.

I drew some consolation from the thought that I'd been placed in charge of a journal of knowledge essential to the Air Force's conduct of the war, helping to make possible the development of its planes, weapons, and all their systems. I repeated to myself that while I was in charge, *The Technical Data Digest* had grown into a journal with abstracts written by some forty leading scientists and read by nearly six thousand Air Force technicians and civilian researchers, including those of all our allies. This, I told myself, this must have counted for something.

True, my duties were essentially civilian in nature, harnessed to military needs. Still it was quite unusual for one as young as I was to have so much responsibility, more than I would ever again be given or seek. It was exciting to witness the sudden advances in aircraft design and performance, in materials and fuels, in instrumentation, and the emergence of helicopters and jet propulsion, as month by month the papers and articles to be abstracted predicted and recorded these progressions. And having met and corresponded with dozens of accomplished scientists and engineers, I had a far better comprehension of the way they thought and worked, of their commitments to pure science as well as to its military applications.

All this followed from the accident of my having had a job that summer between semesters at college. I'd been very lucky indeed to have been assigned to such stimulating work. While learning to perform it I'd had to master unanticipated skills, learn to get along with a mixed lot of ingots in the melting pot of the Army, learn to manage other people's work, how better to make our project fill the needs it was intended to serve, and how to thread my way through the AAF's red tape, a crash course in the stupefying inertia of large organizations.

Most of these proficiencies would have little or limited use in whatever civilian life held for me, but one further demand of my wartime duties would, I knew, stay with me. I had had to learn to write jargon-free, perspicuous, and unambiguous prose; this discipline would be a permanent part of my personal armament and would influence my future in ways I could not then foresee or imagine. Another bonus was my familiarity with editing, layout, publication processes, and printing, knowledge which in later years protected my own writings from the rule-book deformations of copy editors and, until the advent of typesetting by computer, gave me an insider's knowledge of book production. And I had had a range of other experiences, by-blows of where I was and whom I'd known, that could not otherwise have come to me.

★   ★   ★

It was time to look ahead. What would I do when out of uniform? I hadn't finished college, true, but perhaps the experience of the past three years could lead to a civilian career in similar work. But where? All the aeronautical magazines but one were filled with puffery for the products of the manufacturers who supplied military aircraft equipment but were even now retooling for the civilian markets. No way to know, then, that this reduction from military to civilian production would bring on a crisis in the aircraft industry. I had no desire, now that the war was won, to become an editorial slavey for commerce. The exceptional publication was the *Journal of Aeronautical Sciences,* published by the American Society of Aeronautical Engineers. If there was room on their staff for me, I could work in the service of science.

My letter of inquiry and résumé, however, eventually brought me only an offer of an appointment as assistant editor at the princely sum of seventy-five dollars per week. What, start over on the bottom rung? The middle-aged editors of this estimable journal were not about to move over for a whiz-kid soon out of uniform. This response from the *J.A.S.*, which I couldn't accept, blessedly brought me up short. I came to my senses, realized that advancement in any technical writing or editorial career would require advanced degrees in engineering and mastery of mathematics, the very subjects I had found so problematical before entering the service. To handle responsibilities in civilian life comparable to those I had held in service would take years and years of apprenticeship. And why had I been thinking of continuing in this line of work? I now knew that I was not committed, as anyone in the aviation industry in whatever capacity must be, to the concept of inevitable progress.

Progress we had needed every day and in every way while at war. It was the tangible press of technical progress that gave our forces the advanced equipment and weapons needed for victory. Who could but be stirred by the harnessing of scientific knowledge, technical skills, industrial might? But in peacetime, why would technological progress stir my soul? War or no war, the linkage of industry to the military would continue; one could foresee the scramble for contracts, the pressuring of the Congress for endless funding. Such a forecast did not attract me.

What, after all, were the enthusiasms that came like second nature to my nature? I'd been reading poetry much more modern than any taught at college, in the *New Poems 1944* anthology I'd bought in Cincinnati and, more significantly, in Yeats. His poems, with their masterful rhythm, their magisterial involvement in history as well as passionate expression of love and of suffering, made me aware how lamely my own verse limped, how wide were the horizons a poet could aim to embrace. And I'd come on Gerard Manley Hopkins, and was swept away by his pulsing rhythms, the stunning and startling harmonies and dissonances in the sounds of his language and wordplay. Like the tramps in Robert Frost's poem, I'd like to make my avocation my vocation.

Hitherto I'd had to practice it, in my uninstructed way, on stolen time.

And my interest in jazz had grown into a fascination with folklore, especially ballads, blues, and other verbal folk arts that grew out of and reflected communities of experience. In folklore, in the communal experience of verbal and musical art forms, were the roots, the sources of the aesthetic sensibilities that informed great art. I was curious to explore the connections between folk and high art, to see how unlettered people could share and help to create and preserve ballads, songs, tales, musical conventions. Besides, I was taken by the vicarious sense of belonging that immersion in these materials provided. My interests led toward discovering the development of present forms from origins, roots, beginnings; I didn't then articulate the contrast, but these predilections were in fact the opposite of the futurism inherent in technological progress.

Well, I thought, I'd better go back to college and finish my junior year.

The last piece of writing I did at Wright Field was to compose a letter of commendation for all members of *The Technical Data Digest* staff, to be placed, after being signed by Colonel Davis, in their military records or civil service personnel files. A month after my own release from service a commending letter arrived for me, sent to my aunt and uncle's home, my last address before induction. It was signed by Colonel Donald Putt, then Deputy Commanding General, Intelligence, T-2.

★   ★   ★

Newspaper headlines on February 16, 1946, announced that Interior Secretary Eccles opposed higher wages, since they would lead to increased prices. Pope Pius warned the Soviets that his stand against Communism was unalterable. The economy was adjusting to peacetime pressures, the world to the as yet unnamed cold war. My service in the AAF was by now merely time-killing. Even the Air Force realized that.

On that morning, half a dozen of us, junior officers all, were summoned to the office of the Commanding Officer of the

4265th AAF Base Unit, the separation base at Patterson Field, an outfit of whose existence I had been unaware. There we were called forward, each handed a sheet of paper, given a salute, and dismissed with no pomp and less circumstance. From that moment forward, we were civilians again.

My discharge coincided with Leon's release from the infantry—we'd kept in touch while he was in Germany guarding prisoners, then retraining for invasion of Japan; he'd been in the U.S. en route to the Pacific when the atom bomb suddenly ended the war. We decided to celebrate our reentry into civilian life together. So I joined him in Chicago for several nights of carousing with his friends from the Art Institute. Then, borrowing his family's car, we drove across icy farmlands to Iowa City, where his sister's enrollment in the university gave us pretext for a trip. Speeding across frozen cornfields, the highway on a dike, the car hit black ice and skidded out of control down the embankment; after a frozen couple of hours, a farmer with tractor hauled us back to the road. It was an eerie trip, the two of us racketing along those deserted frozen fields, dimly aware that the freedom from Army regimentation we longed for would require some inner discipline of our own.

Back in Chicago, I looked in at the university and attended a lecture by the philosopher Rudolf Carnap, who maintained that sensory experience was all illusory. This was philosophy?—abstract theorizing proved false by real life? I felt a shrinking of my fealty to his field. This period is a bit hazy in retrospect; at its end I departed for New York and what I had managed to keep as much at a distance as possible for the preceding three years, the acrimonious tensions of my disintegrating family.

★　★　★

Once again ensconced in a monastic cell in John Jay Hall, I signed up for summer session courses in poetry of the seventeenth century and introduction to anthropology, the latter as a grounding for the folklore study I planned in the future. Continuing in philosophy no longer appealed; I would complete the two-semester course in the history of philosophy with John Herman Randall that I had started in 1942—the second semester took up just where the first, four years earlier, had ended, as though nothing had happened between them. But my imagination now was stirred more by the ways literature represented, satirized, or transcended life itself: a commitment to the imaginative representation of actual emotions and the concrete details of experience, no longer to abstract theories.

The poetry course was taught by a visiting professor, A. L. Barker of the University of Toronto. I'd come on poems in anthologies by Donne, Marvell, Herbert, and other metaphysicals, but reading them closely, in historical context, was to experience them with a new intensity and comprehension. I was intrigued by the fusion, in Donne, of passion and reasoned argument, by the enriching complexity of his metaphors, the sinuosities of syntax; in Herbert and Marvell, the ease of movement, the seeming naturalness of adaptation of sense to rhyme, meter, and form. These realizations stirred me to attempt emulation, or at least imitation, and once again I got up my nerve to turn in at the end of Barker's course a set of verses modelled on those on the reading list. And again I was in luck, for this professor seemed to be, or to have been, a writer of poems himself; at least, so I inferred from his reception of my efforts in the style of three centuries before the date on my term paper: I was given A–, doubtless more than my verses deserved.

I was well on my way now to a life entirely different from my aeronautical career. Classes were filled with other returned servicemen, all older, more mature, more serious, more committed seminarians and discussants than we'd been in 1941 or '42. Intellectual life was continually exciting. I knew that whatever I did henceforth, I would have to have time to write. College teaching appealed as a good solution—one had some control over how one's time was spent, and the work itself, discussing significant books and poems with interested students and stimulating colleagues, looked attractive. In 1947 one could choose this career on that basis and discover that one's reasons were in fact true.

In the next few years, taking all three degrees at Columbia, I'd study eighteenth century with Joseph Wood Krutch, French literature with Wilbur Frohock, cultural anthropology with Ruth Benedict and Conrad Arensberg, the history of the English language with Elliot V. K. Dobbie, Chaucer and Arthurian romance with Roger Sherman Loomis, seventeenth century with Marjorie Hope Nicholson, American literature with Lionel Trilling, European literature of the past two centuries in a colloquium with Trilling and Jacques Barzun, modern poetry with William York Tindall, and reading poems from all periods in one course and a semester on *Don Quixote* in another with Mark Van Doren. I was exceptionally lucky to be at Columbia at this time, when the intellectual stimulation from this faculty could not have been matched anywhere. This education was heady stuff. The immersion in the traditions of European and American culture made it possible to see how traditions develop and engender the works of genius that represent them, and how some of those works modify the traditions in which they came into being. My sense developed of the continuities of culture, especially of literature. I could see how the history of the language and of the forms and styles of poetry, drama, fiction, all formed an ever-changing continuum, knowledge of which could only enrich one's own writing. This was no merely passive absorption of T. S. Eliot's essays; I had already felt and worked out for myself the sense of continuities within changing artistic traditions, reached as an amateur musicologist tracing the emergence and history of jazz. And I had seen that advances in aeronautical science—helicopters, radial engines, more efficient wing designs, jet propulsion—all emerged from preceding knowledge, a continuum of development. What held true in music and in aviation would be applicable also to the study of language, of literature, of culture. I felt advantaged, too, by my growing confidence in literary analysis, which I could reflexively employ on my own attempts to write, and by continual practice in the forms and meters which make poetry in English so capable of expressing every emotion. I was aware of other poets or would-be poets, the egoistic romanticism of whose responses to modern life made them reject every inherited advantage to their art. For them, contemporary life was aleatoric, unconnected to any past; while for me, tradition was not an imprisoning suit of armor but a fountain of possibilities, enabling present or remembered experience to be illuminated by resonances and depths of historical allusion.

I was studying hard, taking part in editorial meetings, every Tuesday noon in John Jay Hall, of the *Columbia Review,* the literary magazine. I'd supposed that student publications had died out during our absence, but no, they were all alive and flourishing, filled with contributions, under many *noms de plume,* from the typewriter of John Hollander, who'd been too young for Army service. Already a polymath, he was poetry editor and accepted several poems of mine, as well as some by associate editor Allen Ginsberg, who, like me the preceding summer, was writing faux-Donne verses. Also on the *Review* staff was Joe Kraft, later a renowned political columnist. Our board was headed by Norman Kelvin, the future much-praised editor of the letters of William Morris.

I was also writing an essay, "The American Culture and the Creative Personality." Constance Rourke's *American Humor* gave me a context for my musings on folklore. Now I explored the folk arts of a simpler time, colonial America, contrasting the situation of the folk artist then to that of the individual artist in our fragmented industrial culture. Things I had long thought about, even participated in, and could now study, were coming together in my mind. This essay was breaking the ground I'd later explore in four books that investigated the uses of folklore—themes, characters, plots, language, forms—in literary works of first intensity, works by Washington Irving, Hawthorne, Melville, Mark Twain, Yeats, Robert Graves, Edwin Muir, and Faulkner.

★   ★   ★

One hot evening that summer, needing respite from study and the unending dialectical discussions in the dorm, I asked a girl I'd met to go to the movies. She agreed, but on learning that I had in mind a fifteen-year-old foreign film, came down with a sudden headache. So I walked alone down Broadway to the Thalia, the art film–repertoire theater thirty blocks from the campus. There, in emulation of the civilized practice of theaters in Paris and London, was a coffee bar in the lobby and, on the walls, an exhibition of paintings. The feature that night in no way involved reflection on any of my courses. It was *"M" the Kidnapper.*

Among the couples and singles waiting for the next show, a pair of young women across the lobby, who'd evidently come together, caught my eye. Quite apart from their being so attractive, I was curious that they'd chosen to spend the evening here. One looked like a model—statuesque, dark-haired, quite young, and gotten up in a determinedly provocative fashion—sheath dress, purple lipstick and fingernails, perhaps a bit much. The other, more conventionally dressed, had a winsome figure and shoulder-length, chestnut hair and bangs. She wore none of the attention-getting artifices of her companion, yet from across the room, seeing her speak, so amused, intense, and lively, I felt curious, no, strongly attracted. I went over, struck up a conversation, and when let into the theater, searched for seats. I'll not forget the look on the girl with bangs when I said, "Here's a pair together, and there's another right behind us in the next row," steered her companion toward the single, and took the seat beside the one for her. When the film let out I took them both for a drink to a nearby bar on Broadway.

The taller girl, indeed a model, was an art student, not long out of some small town in Ohio. Beneath her now exotic exterior I sensed a very nice person, a more sophisticated version of the poised, good-looking teenagers I'd met at the Dayton Service Club. But it was her friend I found strangely alluring, even though, as we discussed the film, she seemed decidedly dippy. There's no hidden meaning in *"M" the Kidnapper,* no arcane symbolism, yet she had trouble saying anything sensible even about Peter Lorre's superb performance as the obsessed child-abuser hunted down by the brotherhood of the underworld to free themselves from persecution by the police.

Still, when she asked what brought me to the Upper West Side, I sensed that presenting myself only as an English major studying Coffin and Witherspoon's *Seventeenth-Century Poetry* might seem a bit stuffy, so I casually added, "I had a lucky break yesterday—down on Lower Broadway, browsing in bookstores, at the Strand I found Oscar Williams's anthology *New Poems 1940.* I already had the volume for 1944." Then, to appear really avant-garde, I asked, "You must know these anthologies?"

"Oh yes, I have *New Poems 1942* and *1943.* I've been looking for the others."

What serendipity! "Oh, we must exchange books—I'll lend you mine." We lingered in that tatty bar on Broadway, finding one after another thing on which we agreed, opinions shared, music we both enjoyed—although she was not yet acquainted with jazz, I'd met no other girl in New York who'd even heard of "Variations on a Theme by Thomas Tallis." Her conversation had hints of humor, of irony. Skeptical of received verities, she had the tinge of an untamable spirit challenging conventionality, yet was unmistakably a romantic. I couldn't believe my luck!

Her pretty companion, thoughtlessly shunted aside, looked a bit forlorn. I walked them back to Ferguson, an Episcopal women's residence on West 87th Street, and made a date to take the one I favored to the Thalia the following Saturday. The feature would be the silent classic *Le Dernier Testament de Docteur M'Abuse,* a treatment, daring for its time, of fascism as a madman's dream. No love story, that, but a chance to see such a great film could not be missed.

This time it was just the two of us. When we got to the Thalia, the opening frames on screen revealed a change of the bill. Instead we'd see *The Cabinet of Dr. Caligari.* Some booking clerk had confused the two cans with "Dr." in their titles. Again after the show we went to the bar on Broadway. She was eager to discuss the film—Dr. M'Abuse represented Hitler, and the final scene, with him wild-eyed in an asylum cutting a string of paper dolls, symbolized the dehumanization of totalitarianism . . . Good Lord, I thought, she couldn't have seen the screen and didn't know we were watching *Dr. Caligari* instead—hadn't seen the movie either time!

Gently, I suggested that her account of *Docteur M'Abuse,* while insightful, had little relevance to the film actually shown. Then, embarrassed, she confessed to being so nearsighted she had to wear glasses but hated the way her specs looked and didn't want to show herself in their unbecoming frames. Knowing that of course I'd want to discuss the picture, she'd gone on her lunch hours to the Museum of Modern Art Film Library and boned up on the show we'd expected to see. She pulled out of her handbag a pair of round horn-rims. Touched, I assured her I enjoyed being with her so much I hoped to see her again and again, with or without her glasses. Well, I was determined not to let *this* one get away.

After bidding her goodnight, I returned to Columbia along Riverside Drive, where the whole night sky gleamed with re-flected light, repeating to myself over and over her name. What was the conjunction of the invisible stars, here in New York where there are millions of chance encounters every day, that had brought me last week to the Thalia on the same night and at the same time that Elizabeth McFarland had gone to see the same show? In the excitement of the moment all this was tumbling through my head—could I win and keep this girl who, more than anyone I'd known, filled the portrait I hadn't till then known I carried in my mind?

To put these impressions and feelings into perspective, let me skip ahead some years. Here's an effort to record a more ripened experience of these encounters and some of their consequences, a perspective that still holds true:

> As I was going to Saint-Ives
> In stormy, windy, sunny weather
> I meet a man with seven wives
> (The herons stand in the swift water).
>
> One drinks her beer out of his can
> In stormy, windy, and bright weather,
> And who laughs more, she or her man?
> (The herons stand still on the water.)
>
> One knows the room his candle lit
> In stormy, lightning, cloudburst weather,
> That glows again at the thought of it
> (Two herons still the swift water).
>
> His jealous, wild-tongued Wednesday's wife—
> In dreepy, wintry, wind-lashed weather

—What rends him like that ranting strife?
(Two herons still the roaring water.)

There's one whose mind's so like his mind
In streaming wind or balmy weather
All joy, all wisdom seem one kind
(The herons stand in the swift water.)

And one whose secret mazes he
In moon-swept, in torrential weather
Ransacks, and cannot find the key
(Two herons stand in the white water).

He'll think of none save one's slim thighs
In heat and sleet and windy weather
Till death has plucked his dreaming eyes
(Two herons guard the streaming water).

And the one whose love moves all he's done,
In windy, warm, and wintry weather,
—What can he leave but speaks thereon?
Two herons still the swift water.

From an article by the poet Lewis Turco I learned a lot about my ballad's prosody, and also that many young readers these days may never have heard of the traditional riddle I took for granted as point of departure. I had revelled in the possibilities offered by the opening rhyme of the riddle, and chose the ballad form as, with the riddle, among the most archaic literary forms in the language. The images and feelings in the poem are indeed personal, but I wished to express them not as unique: I'd give them their due in the recurring rhythms of life, as ours in the repertoire of experiences long and widely shared.

In the riddle, each wife had seven cats, each cat had seven kits, etc., till it's asked, How many were going to Saint-Ives? Assuming all were met as they came *from* Saint-Ives, the answer is one. Although in my ballad the encounter is seen differently, the implied riddle's answer is the same. The man met by the traveller—his shadow-self, his double—is going, as he is, toward Land's End, that is, life's end, helping him, as they go together, recognize and rejoice in the multiple realities of his wife and her relationship to him. The refrain poses against our ever-changeful water and weather a pair of herons, who may, as Lew Turco suggests, represent ourselves, yet are the real, noble birds we'd often seen on the shores of Cape Rosier, Maine. There they were perhaps unaware of their ancient significance as symbols of regeneration and immortality.

These may seem heavy burdens for a mere ballad, but despite the fraying of what was once our common culture, I reach for such allusions to give resonance to actual experiences and thus deepen the expression of real emotions.

★　★　★

One day I pulled out of my dormitory mailbox a letter forwarded from my aunt and uncle's house in New Rochelle. The return address was Headquarters, Mitchell Field. What was this, a recall to active duty? No, it was an invitation to a ceremony at that base, on October 4. Mitchell Field is in Garden City, and as my parents insisted on coming—only this could bring them together—we went in my father's car, with me in front, my mother and Liz, by now my fiancée, in the back seat.

On arrival we were directed to a large room where a dozen or so other veterans were already waiting. The presence also of their preening parents made them seem as uncomfortable as I was made by mine. At last a colonel strode to the podium between massed flags, welcomed everyone, and began to read the citations for belatedly awarded Purple Hearts, Air Medals, Oak Leaf Clusters, Bronze and Silver Stars. Each honoree came forward, was handed by a captain the leather-covered case containing his medal, then given his citation and a handshake by the colonel. I was called up for a Legion of Merit—the other medallists looked puzzled, nor had I heard of it either. This felt like a summons from an earlier life. At least it indicated that someone up high had noticed what we were doing on the *Digest* and had thought the effort worthwhile.

As it had seemed to everyone at Wright Field, if not at the Pentagon, *The Technical Data Digest*—or at any rate the survey of technological progress it offered—would soon enough be needed, as much for the cold war as for the war just won. What no one in Technical Information could have foreseen was that our *Digest* would be superseded by the fruits of a technological advance it had not been in our purview to follow. While we were typing thousands of abstracts on scores of aeronautical subjects, a couple of engineers at the University of Pennsylvania— John W. Mauchly and J. Prosper Eckert, Jr.—were at work on a completely different problem: devising a mechanism to perform instantaneous calculations for artillery trajectories. They hooked up thousands of vacuum tubes, resistors, capacitors, and switches in a huge, ungainly contraption called the Electronic Numerical Integrator and Computer. It occupied a whole 30-by-50-foot room. (This was in the building adjacent to Bennett Hall, site of the English department, where I held seminars and had an office for twenty-six years.) ENIAC was the first successful anticipation of the digital computer. Within a few years it would be miniaturized, made thousands of times more powerful, and spread its new technology across all fields of research. When the postwar Air Force realized that it again needed a comprehensive survey of current research—doubtless no one involved in that decision had any memory, or had even heard, of *The Technical Data Digest*—the task would be done on computers.

The very method of our magazine was history. A printed compendium of technical abstracts would now be as obsolete as clay tablets incised in cuneiform.

★   ★   ★

Toward the end of my senior year, the Boar's Head Society, our club of student poets, invited W. H. Auden to read to us. In those days colleges didn't invite living poets to do anything, so we took this initiative (and provided the hundred-dollar fee) independently of the English department. One evening about fifteen of us gathered in Earl Hall to hear Auden. Liz was eager to see the great man herself. One of the talented high school kids who corresponded with her at *Scholastic Magazine*—she was now its poetry editor—had excitedly called on her to tell of his meeting with Auden in the poet's flat on St. Mark's Place. Why, we had to wonder, would Auden invite a visit from a mere high school boy? Whatever the answer to that, on his asking Mr. Auden how do poems get written, Robert Thom told her, the great poet had furrowed his brow, leaned back, then, after a pause, said, "The language is the mother . . . the poet is the father . . . and from their union comes the poem."

Since the Boar's Head Society members were all male—not for another thirty years would Columbia go coed—Lizzie put her hair up under a cap and wore trousers and, although the evening was warm, a trench coat. Deceiving none of the student-poets attending, I smuggled her into the meeting. We sat around waiting nervously until, nearly an hour after the expected time, Auden arrived, looking rumpled, his face already as lined as the map of Iceland. He settled into a high-backed chair, extracted from a battered manila envelope some frayed and crumpled sheets of paper, and read a number of poems we'd recently seen in *The New Yorker*.

When he fell silent after our applause, one of the young hopefuls asked the inevitable question: "Mr. Auden, where do poems come from?" To this query our guest paused, looked pensive, furrowed his brow, leaned back, and, putting his pencil to his lips, said, as though conceiving it for the first time, "You must think of the language as the mother . . . the poet as the father . . . and it is their creative union that brings forth the poem."

Neither he nor we knew that among his auditors that night were two he would within the decade choose for the Yale Series of Younger Poets. The other was John Hollander.

★   ★   ★

I'd registered again with the campus employment office, in hopes of supplementing my G.I. Bill allowance with part-time work, and was invited for an interview by the Columbia University Press. They'd seen my résumé and had on offer a job as assistant editor in charge of their King's Crown Press, a subsidiary devised to produce books from doctoral dissertations at the authors' cost (publication was then required for the degree). As such studies had no market other than a few university libraries, they were produced without subjecting the manuscripts to the usual painstaking editorial revision given to maturer works of scholarship.

The Press seemed eager to have me take on this burden, although, as Henry Wiggins, the director, told me, I'd have to give up thought of doing graduate work myself. Fortunately I declined this opportunity, for soon the state universities of Michigan and Wisconsin, finding their doctoral candidates unable to subvene publication, decreed that microfilming would serve equally well. This was a saving for the student of a couple of thousand dollars. All other universities soon followed suit, and Columbia closed its King's Crown imprint.

In the event, my dissertation, *The Poetry of Stephen Crane,* was published by Columbia in 1957. It evidently qualified as mature scholarship enough; my master's essay, on the folklore, popularizations, and literary treatments of Paul Bunyan, had been published in 1952. I'd undertaken these compositional requirements not as cobbling footnoted essays to please a committee, but conceived as books in the making.

Organizing and writing expository prose came easily enough, but every time I tried to write poems there was the struggle to discover my own voice. While learning how other poets used the language, imagery, metaphor, sound pattern, form, syntax—all the constituent elements of poems—there was still the need to reconstitute these lessons in a manner not derivative of theirs. I had a drawer filled with a hundred poems I'd thought complete but had come to realize were false starts. At last, though, I was writing a couple of the poems I'd be confident enough to include in my first book. Cultural contexts, verse techniques, the resonances of diction—all these could be learned. My humanistic education at Columbia primed my mind with possibilities. What remained to be discovered were the ways inner necessity would compel expression.

The earliest theme I found means to speak with some distinctiveness was cited by Auden in his foreword to my first book, *An*

Armada of Thirty Whales, in 1954, several years later. Auden wrote, "The poet today is faced not only with the question of contemporary expression but also with the task of recovering the feeling which he and the public have largely lost, that Nature is numinous. . . . [Mr. Hoffman does not] try to pretend to a Wordsworthian intimacy with Nature. He knows that, for any member of our urban culture, such intimacy is not given but is a prize slowly and patiently to be won." One of the poems in *An Armada* in which I tried to offer such recognition of the numinous is this one, based on my having heard, often in the Maine woods, the song of a reclusive bird, the more vividly remembered on hearing a recording from the Cornell Ornithological Laboratory broadcast during the intermission of *Lucia di Lammermoor* for comparison to the soprano's "Mad Song":

The voice of the woodthrush played at half speed

    reveals to the halting ear
    the fullstopt organ that pours through floodgate reed
    such somersaults of sound like waters falling
    in dark crystal chambers
    on iron timbrels

    withholds from what we hear
    those haunting basses, loud but too deepkeyed.
    This slow bisected bird's yet wilder calling
    resounds on inward anvil:
    pain is mortal, mortal.

The sentence in Auden's foreword most heartening to me was this: "While admitting the pains and tragedies of life, he can find joy in life and say so." Part of that joy is in the completion of feeling and the ordering of unmediated experience in form. Another part is in finding the language irreplaceable for its function in the poem. Aeronautical writing had taught me the uses of unambiguous clarity; now poetry sometimes demanded the ambiguities, the hidden ramifications of associations and meanings in words. Reading Emerson's "Nature," I understood when he told us that all words were once metaphors, that language itself is fossil poetry.

No matter how experienced, in poetry one is ever an apprentice, ever hoping for the imaginative leap of vision that will embody feeling and thought in language adequate to its inescapable occasion. Some thirty years after "The voice of the woodthrush" I tried to define the mysterious process by which experience, all that one has done and known, is sifted until one is given the language and form adequate to express the inner compulsion that brought the poem into being:

The Poem

Arriving at last,

It has stumbled across the harsh
Stones, the black marshes.

True to itself, by what craft
And strength it has, it has come
As a sole survivor returns

From the steep pass.
Carved on Memory's staff
The legend is nearly decipherable.
It has lived up to its vows

If it endures
The journey through the dark places
To bear witness,
Casting its message
In a sort of singing.

To discover those legends, in the sites of joy as well as in the dark places, and to set down the messages given there, would require a lifetime's further exploration of the zone of the interior.

Afterthought

W RITING a memoir requires of its author a double consciousness. One presents oneself as one was at the time described, but that self is inevitably conditioned by the self one is at
the time of writing—a different person. This second self strives
for total recall, hoping for honesty in the presentation despite the
perhaps unavoidable tendency to re-create the former self in the
best light, nor can it help but judge its predecessor. Looking back
after over half a century, conditioned now by a lifetime's accu-
mulated experience, knowledge, and self-knowledge, one's view
of the youth one was cannot help but be tinged with regret at
chances missed, opportunities not taken, ambitions and ideals
unrealized. These self-reservations can be among the nearly decipherable legends carved on the staff on which a poet leans as
he walks both back into his past and forward toward his future. I
hope this will be evident in a poem, written in 1971, halfway in
time between what this memoir records and the present in
which it was written.

Vows

I meet him in the spaces
Between the half-familiar places
Where I have been.
It's when I'm struggling toward the door
Of the flooded cellar
Up to my crotch in a cold soup
Of my father's ruined account books
There, like an oyster cracker,
Floats my mother's Spode tureen
(The one they sold at auction
When the market was down)—

Then just outside
Before I'm on the trooptrain on the siding
Spending the vivid years
Of adolescence and the war
With dented messkit in hand
Always at the end
Of a frozen chowline
Of unappeased hungers,
He appears—

Listen, kid,
Why do you bug me with your reproachful
Silent gaze—
What have I ever
Done to you but betray you?
To which he says
Nothing.

Listen, I'd forget if I could
Those plans you made
For stanching the blood
Of the soul that spread
Its cry for peace across the unjust sky,
I wouldn't give it a thought if I

Could only not
Remember your vows
To plunge into the heat
Of the heart and fuse
With the passionate Word
All thought,
All art—

Come, let's go together
Into the burning
House with its gaping door.
The windows are all alight
With the color of my deeds,
My omissions.
It's our life that's burning.
Is it ever too late to thrust
Ourselves into the ruins,
Into the tempering flame?